Horseplay on the Front Lawn

Memories of 2 Benedict Street

Peg Crist McCloskey

Horseplay on the Front Lawn

Copyright © 2019 - Peg Crist McCloskey

Formatting: Wild Seas Formatting (http://www.WildSeasFormatting.com)

ISBN: 978-1-6727-5565-8

Contents

Preface

This story of our family was written in loving memory of my parents. It is intended as nothing more than a resource of family information for the descendants of Margaret Dennin Crist and Robert Michael Crist. This effort has been a marvelous trip down memory lane for me. I have loved hearing stories from others in the family and have learned much about our family's history during my research.

I have presented, as best I can, the history of the family lines from which my brothers and I and succeeding generations descend. In researching and writing this story, I felt a sense of awe at the challenges so many of our forefathers—and foremothers—endured during their lifetimes. I make no claim to be a talented writer and apologize for any errors or incorrect information. In many cases, spellings of names, and dates of birth and/or death, for our oldest ancestors differed slightly depending on the source of information such as the New York State Census, cemetery records, Albany City Directories, obituaries or even Ancestry.com. I did my best to make sense of the differences, but there may be room to quibble with my final decisions in some cases. Additionally, it is more than likely that new information will become available as family members continue their research. I eagerly await new findings. This information will be added to my efforts through electronic or other means through the years. Lastly, several remarkable "coincidences" found their way into the story. See how many you can find.

There were many family stories to relate—stories that

were told and retold during my childhood and beyond. My brothers and I each have our own memories. They recall things I don't remember and, what we all remember, we sometimes remember differently. And some memories are private, never to be shared.

My hope is to preserve our family history for future generations. For some readers, there may be more details and/or stories than you care to stay with. But this is the story of who we are, where our roots were formed, and what our lives have been like. Read what you wish, and it is my hope that what you read will aid you in knowing more about yourself and, more importantly, the sacrifices that were made on our behalf by those who have passed before us.

This daughter, mother, sister, niece, aunt and cousin of the family members who star in our story has spent a lifetime feeling enormously proud and thankful to have been part of our family. Growing up in 1940s and 1950s Castleton provided a sense of security, belonging, and comfort that has never left me and which, I fear, many young people today will never experience. I loved sitting on the front porch of 2 Benedict Street in the cool dusk of a summer's evening, with a million stars overhead and fireflies flickering nearby; listening to the soulful sound of a steam whistle as the train rumbled in the distance; watching a boat creep silently past on the Hudson River with its lights dancing on the water just beyond the railroad tracks; and having the comfortable companionship of family and friends—life was good. Life was in order. Life was secure. That sense of security has stayed with me my entire life and has sustained me. And I am so grateful to have had these experiences.

Creating this book has been a goal throughout much of my adult lifetime and it has been a joy to accomplish. I am thrilled to present it.

And so, with apologies to the "Lone Ranger," I invite you to return with me now to those thrilling days of yesteryear. I hope you will enjoy your story.

Part One

The Dennins

The Dennin Family Line

Note: Making sense of generations of family history can be notoriously difficult. To make our history less complicated, I have put together what I call barebones family trees (pun intended) for the **Dennins** and the **Crists**. These can serve as a quick reference as you read through the detailed histories of our ancestors.

THE DENNIN FAMILY LINE

PATRICK DENNIN, SR.
B: 1790 Ireland
D: after 1855 Albany, New York

PATRICK DENNIN, JR.
B: 1831 Ireland
D: 1881 Albany, New York

THOMAS DENNIN
B: Ireland
D:

WILLIAM W. DENNIN
B: 1857 Albany, New York
D: 1918 Albany, New York

BRIDGET DENNIN
B: 1827 Ireland
D: 1912 Albany, New York

ELIZABETH REYNOLDS
B: Ireland
D:

MARGARET ELIZABETH DENNIN
B: 1905 Albany, New York
D: 1971 Castleton on Hudson

FIRST WIFE
MARY CURLEY
B: 1860 Ireland
D: 1893 Albany, New York

TIMOTHY O'SULLIVAN
B: About 1808 Ireland
D:

MICHAEL P. O'SULLIVAN
B: 1842 Ireland
D: 1913 Albany, New York

MARGARET CONNORS
B: 1813 Ireland

MARGARET ELIZABETH O'SULLIVAN
B: 1870 Albany, New York
D: 1964 Albany, New York

ELIZABETH SMITH
B: 1843 Ireland
D: 1919 Albany, New York

It has been said that one's life is all about when, where, and to whom you were born.

Patrick Dennin Jr.
My Maternal Great-grandfather (Paternal Side)

Mid-twentieth century Ireland was a vibrant and prosperous country boasting scenic coastal areas, abundant seafood, bountiful grazing areas, majestic lakes, verdant landscapes, picturesque inns, and quaint folklore. The Irish are known to be a joyous people who celebrate life with their dancing, music, and love of family.

A hundred years earlier Ireland presented a very different face. Its impoverished lower class consisted of mostly Irish Catholic farmers who had little hope of improving their lot. The country's fisheries were undeveloped, and the nation had yet to be industrialized. Catholics made up about eighty percent of the population of about eight million inhabitants.

The ruling British government held the Irish in very low regard, considering them lazy and stupid. Catholics were badly discriminated against in mid-nineteenth century Ireland and did not have the right to vote, attend school, hold any government positions or become lawyers. Additionally, it was extremely difficult to become a landowner due to a variety of laws aimed at Catholics. Land was largely held by wealthy absentee Anglo-Irish owners who leased small parcels to rural peasant farmers to grow their crops, establish an abode, and feed their families. This system dictated that peasants would never be prosperous enough to own land on a par with the Protestants. Rental payments on the home and land were made from the sale of harvested potatoes, grain and oats, as well as the sale of animals such as pigs and poultry.

Potatoes—rich in vitamins and minerals—were also grown to feed the family throughout the year. The possession of a rented plot of productive farmland often meant the difference between life and death for the impoverished.

The hardships placed upon many Irish Catholics dictated that they live in stone or earthen huts with dirt floors. Often the huts did not have windows or chimneys. Smoke created from burning peat for cooking, or for keeping the hut warm, was vented through a hole in the thatched roof. Landlords did not permit the entry door to be higher than five feet eight inches. Tenants often created a step down into the ground inside the door to allow for more interior height. Any improvements to the hut by the tenant brought about a rise in the rental fee.

Household goods consisted of sparse furnishings with bedding sometimes laid on the ground or perhaps on top of straw. Often a pig and/or poultry shared the hut with the family. Meals consisted largely of boiled potatoes with salt and milk. Cabbage, fish, and the occasional dairy product rounded out their diet. Even in these primitive conditions, the farmers and their families were able to keep warm with readily available peat to burn. They kept an upbeat attitude, but there was always a waiting game to see if the current crop of potatoes would last until the next crop could be harvested to keep their stomachs full.

Young women often married by sixteen while young men were seventeen or eighteen when they wed. And the Irish believed in large families. A family of eight or nine children was not unusual. However, limited medical care meant the survival rate for infants and young children was very low.

The population of Ireland hit an all-time peak of around 8,200,000 inhabitants in 1841. Two million of that number were peasant farmers and their dependents. It was into this land that my **maternal great-grandfather Patrick Dennin Jr.** was born in 1831 in Longford in Leinster Province in the Midlands region of Ireland.

Patrick was the son of **Patrick Dennin Sr**. who was born in Ireland in 1790.

***

The Great Potato Famine which began in 1845 and lasted until 1849 was a calamitous event in Ireland and is ranked in the top ten greatest famines ever to occur in the world. In 1845 the potato crop throughout Ireland developed blight and about a third of the crop was a failure.

The winter of 1846-47 was extremely harsh with heavy snow and an icy northeast wind from Russia which brought bitterly cold temperatures. The Irish were accustomed to a much more moderate winter climate. Further, three-quarters of the 1846 potato crop was a failure and brought no relief to the shortage of food. Over the next four-year period, millions of peasants who lived largely on potatoes suddenly faced starvation, and more than one million people succumbed to excruciating deaths. Tenants were cruelly evicted from their huts into the frigid Irish winter for non-payment of rent. Following eviction, their humble homes were destroyed so they couldn't return. For many, especially the elderly or the infirm, there was no refuge to be found and death awaited.

Hundreds of men, women, and children died in the streets weekly, following eviction. Beggars were found in many areas throughout the country, especially in the western counties of Galway, Sligo, and Mayo.

"Famine fever," which included dysentery, diarrhea, and tuberculosis, claimed tens of thousands. Typhus and cholera were also epidemic among the population. As horrendous as the famine was, disease killed far more people than the famine.

The ruling British government attempted various methods to aid the starving masses through soup kitchens, workhouses, public works projects and importation of (largely inedible) Indian corn from the

United States. Charitable groups throughout the world donated food and money, but none of these efforts were particularly effective. The British refused to intervene more aggressively to aid the starving people. Much of the locally grown food was exported to England or continental Europe with the policy of laissez-faire (free trade). Had the exported food been kept in Ireland, along with effective government assistance to the poor, the famine would have been greatly alleviated. The British rulers continued to hold the Irish partially responsible for this cataclysm, citing their nature of being lazy. The British, failing in their attempts to provide sufficient aid, ultimately pronounced the famine to be the work of God.

In 1997 British Prime Minister Tony Blair apologized to the Irish people for his country's failure to alleviate the famine. For a further understanding of the horrors that took place during the Irish famine, many of which are too gruesome to report here, and England's role in that tragedy, my nephew Gary Crist recommends noted Irish historian Tim Pat Coogan's definitive book *The Famine Plot* published in 2012. My take-away from reading Coogan's work is that those of us who descend from Patrick Dennin are most fortunate to have been born.

***

A mass emigration of Irish who sought a better life in the New World began in 1846. More than a quarter of the Irish population emigrated or died during the Great Famine years. Most Irish emigrants were confident about the three-hour voyage across the Irish Sea to the port in Liverpool, believing the short voyage would be safe and food would be available in England. The longer voyage from Liverpool to Canada or America held much more uncertainty.

Rickety, unsanitary, and barely navigable sailing vessels left Ireland from ports such as Galway, Cork and Dublin and landed in Canada, New York, Boston, Philadelphia or New Orleans and even Australia, among others. A voyage from County Cork, via Liverpool, to New York in 1849 cost about seven pounds for an adult (an unimaginable amount for the impoverished). There were two classes of travel: standard or steerage. Unspeakable and horrific conditions prevailed on the multi-week voyage, especially in steerage class. Passengers, many of whom were already sick with typhus, were herded like animals into the dark and dank crammed decks below, where food, clean water and sanitation were in very low supply. The ships became known as "coffin ships" because so many of the destitute immigrants did not survive the voyage.

Gary Crist provided a manifest which shows that a **Patrick Dennin** traveled from Ireland to Boston via Liverpool aboard the *Plymouth Rock*. Patrick's ship landed in Boston on May 9, 1850. The Patrick Dennin on the manifest is listed as being nineteen years old. This would be in keeping with a birth date of 1831 that we have for Patrick Dennin, Jr. Patrick couldn't have known upon his departure in the spring of 1850 at age nineteen that the fall potato crop of 1850 would be healthy and bring an end to the five-year Irish famine.

We can only speculate on Patrick Jr.'s circumstances prior to his leaving Ireland; however, the fact that Patrick wasn't in the earliest wave of émigrés may indicate they were people of some means. Or perhaps he stayed to care for ailing or elderly family members. It is doubtful that we will ever know Patrick's story before leaving Ireland. Although we don't know when Patrick Senior immigrated to the New World, father and son ultimately reconnected in Albany, New York. Patrick Dennin Sr. was listed in the 1855 New York State census as being a sixty-five-year-old widower and living at the 111 Orange Street home of his son.

***

Patrick Jr. survived the long and difficult voyage, but upon arrival found that life, while better than Ireland, would not be easy in the New World. Having landed in Boston, along with many thousands of his countrymen, Patrick eventually made his way to Albany, a city founded by the Dutch 200 years earlier and a destination of choice for many Irish immigrants. He would have had very few personal possessions beyond basic necessities.

Albany was settled in 1610 and was the second major settlement in the New World, following the establishment of a settlement at Jamestown in Virginia in 1607. British King William III and Queen Mary II jointly ruled the Dutch settlers beginning in 1664 and established the rule of law regarding commerce with the native Indian population. By the mid-1800's, the city had a population of around 50,000 people as it had become a transportation and manufacturing hub and was a haven for job-seekers. Depending on what money he had available to bring from Ireland, Patrick's first accommodations may have been in the basement of a tenement building in Albany's "Irish Quarter", with no bathrooms or running water. Rooms were dirty and cramped, lit by kerosene lamps, and contained multiple people sharing the small space.

Irish Catholic immigrants were not accepted warmly into largely Protestant America. Local residents feared the Irish would take their jobs and change the culture in unacceptable ways. John Francis McCloskey (no relation) was the first Bishop of the Roman Catholic Diocese of Albany and was instrumental in establishing parochial schools in the city's five Catholic churches. Some of these schools were tuition-funded; the proceeds of which were used to finance the free schools. First generation Irish immigrants had a high mortality rate as a result of the treacherous crossings, typhoid, and other diseases. Bishop McCloskey also established orphanages to provide homes and education for the growing orphan population in the city. The church encouraged the formation of benevolent societies to offer immediate shelter and food to the immigrants.

Integrating into American society or workplaces was

difficult at best for the new settlers. Signs in many businesses read "Irish Not Welcome." Help Wanted ads in newspapers consistently carried the disclaimer "No Irish Need Apply." By 1860 native Irish or first-generation Irish made up forty percent of Albany's population. Two years after arriving in Albany, Patrick Jr. had found steady employment as a carpenter and lived at 103 Orange Street, a three-story brick building.

Life in Albany was made somewhat easier with establishments such as Blasie's Shaving and Hair Dressing Rooms on 389 Broadway where a man could have a hot bath and shave for twenty-five cents. On Wednesdays and Saturdays, farmers came to town in horse-drawn carriages to sell home-grown produce. The carriages were parked side by side on the cobblestones of State Street. This practice continued until 1890 when the open-air markets were moved to a less conspicuous area south of Eagle Street following the completion of the new Capitol Building on State Street.

Bridget Mary Dennin
My Maternal Great-grandmother (Paternal Side)

Bridget Dennin was the daughter of **Elizabeth Reynolds** and **Thomas Dennin** and was born in Ireland in March of 1827. Like Patrick, she had also immigrated to the New World to escape the conditions in Ireland. It is possible that Bridget and Patrick knew each other in Ireland or that they met in Boston upon arriving in the U.S. Or they may have been cousins! It was not unheard of in this era for cousins to marry. Bridget may have patronized the Turkish baths at 714 Broadway which were exclusively open for women from 8 a.m. to 1 p.m.

By 1851 Patrick and Bridget married and took up residence at 103 Orange Street. Patrick became a naturalized citizen of the United States on October 28, 1858 at the age of twenty-seven. They lived at several different addresses (103, 151, 177) on Orange Street before moving to their permanent residence at 111 Orange Street. Patrick and Bridget eventually became the parents of nine children:

> James (1852 – 1933) died at age eighty-one; Mary E., (1853 – 1857) died at age four; John, born in 1855; **William Wilford Dennin**, (my maternal grandfather) born September 26, 1857 (whose story will be told in the coming pages); Martha, (1858 – 1872) died at age 14; Michael, (1862 – 1886) died at age 24; Joseph, (1863 – 1915) died at age 52; Catherine, (1864 – 1929) died at age 65; and Frank, (1866 – 1916) died at age 50. [Author's note: in researching dates of birth and death for our senior ancestors, the data is not consistent. Relying on census information doesn't always work as different census years sometimes show different dates of birth for the same person. In the case of William W. Dennin, I found three different dates of birth. For purposes of this story, in collaboration with Gary Crist, I have chosen 1857 as the date most likely to be accurate. I have used this same methodology throughout.]

Patrick and Bridget defied the odds as immigrants and made a successful life raising their family together in Albany until tragedy struck suddenly at 5:30 A.M. on October 2, 1881. The October 3 issue of the *Albany Morning Express* describes Patrick's stunning and unexpected death while at work as an "oiler and tester of car wheels" at the nearby New York Central and Hudson River Railroad Company. The large headline read:

"Ground to Atoms—

Shocking Accident at the Union Depot—An Old Employe (sic) Instantly Killed—What was Caused by a Misplaced Switch"

The story detailed the accident in graphic and

gruesome language and went on to describe the deceased: *"Patrick had been in the employ of the company for over 30 years, and was known as a sober, industrious man, being well liked by all. He leaves a wife and five grown up children, consisting of three sons and two daughters."* [Note: We believe the *Morning Express* story about leaving three sons and two daughters behind was incorrect. We count five sons and one daughter left behind].

Patrick's funeral was held at St. Mary's Church on Lodge Street in Albany. The church stands today and is noted for its superb architectural details throughout and is listed in the National Register of Historical Places.

Bridget Dennin outlived four of her nine children and her husband. She lived an additional thirty-one years after Patrick's death and died at the age of eighty-five at the 111 Orange Street home on March 31, 1912 of "exhaustion." Bridget was the first of several of our ancestors to live as a widow or widower for decades.

***

Please pay close attention as you are about to read of a most remarkable coincidence. Gary Crist and Heidi Crist Silvestri's research into family history revealed that following Bridget Dennin's death in 1912 at 111 Orange Street, a gentleman by the name of William Wasserbach moved into the home shortly thereafter. Mr. Wasserbach was a widower with three sons, one of whom was William Wasserbach, Jr. William Jr. married and fathered a daughter by the name of Janet. Janet eventually married Richard Crist—my brother—and they became parents of five children, including Gary and Heidi. To paraphrase Rick in *Casablanca*, "Of all the houses in all the towns in all the world, what are the odds?"

Michael O'Sullivan
My Maternal Great-grandfather (Maternal Side)

Michael O'Sullivan was born in Ireland in January of 1842 to Timothy O'Sullivan (b: 1808) and Margaret Connors (b: 1813) just prior to the Great Potato Famine. Like Patrick and Bridget Dennin, Michael's family, too, fled Ireland in search of a better life in Albany. Michael was a teacher for many years in Albany and later became a proprietor of a book shop. Ultimately, he became a grocer.

Elizabeth Smith
My Maternal Great-grandmother (Maternal Side)

Elizabeth Smith, known as Betsey, was born in Ireland in 1843 and immigrated with her family to Albany where she married Michael O'Sullivan. They had six children: Mary (1868 – 1925) who became a nurse; **Margaret** (my grandmother) (1870 – 1964); John (1872 -1892); Anna (1875 – 1961); Tim born in 1884 and later the father of Wilson, Victor and Bessie Sullivan; and Joseph (1877 – 1892).

Margaret Elizabeth O'Sullivan
My Maternal Grandmother (Maternal Side)

Margaret Elizabeth O'Sullivan, born on December 6, 1870, was the second child of Michael and Elizabeth O'Sullivan. The family made their home at 163 Elm Street in the heart of Albany and just a short walk to the location of the future Capitol Building.

Margaret's father, Michael, was the owner of a small neighborhood butcher shop and grocery at 1112 Broadway at the Albany/Menands City line (the building is no longer there). Cousin Joanne Braun remembered hearing that Grandma worked for her father before her marriage. Michael's parents, Timothy and Margaret, also lived with Michael and his family at 1112 Broadway according to the 1880 census. Margaret's sister, Anna, earned a living as a dress maker. Irish grocers in the mid to late 1800s were known to do well with the large community of immigrants as customers. As the children of an Irish grocer, Margaret and her siblings undoubtedly led a fairly comfortable life while growing up in Albany and there was always plenty to eat.

***

At one point, the New York Central railroad line ran right down the middle of Broadway, past Michael's grocery, and made a stop at the well-known Delavan House which stood for forty years before a devastating fire destroyed it on New Year's Eve of 1894. Sixteen people died in the fire which made headlines throughout the country. Legislators and prominent visitors to the Capitol often stayed at the Delavan House when the State Legislature was in Session. Union Station was later built where the Delavan House had stood. Its doors first opened in December of 1900 to great acclaim. The station's interior was elegant, and the decorative gilded ceiling was especially noted for its beauty.

(A historical note from William Kennedy's *O Albany!* describes President-elect Abraham Lincoln's overnight stop in 1861 at the Delavan House on Broadway. An acclaimed actor by the name of John Wilkes Booth was staying just down the street at Stanwix Hall. Booth was performing as the villainous Pescara in *The Apostate*. Booth was believed to have watched as the *"bearded and stovepipe-hatted Lincoln passed in a horse-drawn carriage in front of Stanwix Hall as the procession headed down Broadway and up State Street en route to the State Capitol."* Kennedy wonders in his book if Lincoln and Booth may have made eye contact as the procession passed Stanwix Hall. As history records, four years later, Booth took Lincoln's life at Ford's Theater in Washington, D.C.)

Both great-grandparents, Michael and Elizabeth,

were gifted with long lives—far exceeding the expected life span of their era. Michael O'Sullivan died in Albany in 1913 of a cerebral hemorrhage at the age of seventy-one. Elizabeth lived for a time with her daughter Margaret's family on Elm Street following Michael's death. She died of nephritis in 1919 at age seventy-six.

William Wilford Dennin, Jr.
My Maternal Grandfather (Paternal Side)

William W. Dennin, the third-born son of Patrick and Bridget, stayed at the 111 Orange Street home with his mother and several siblings for about three years after the death of his father, Patrick, in 1881. William worked in various local businesses as a clerk or an accountant and without question contributed to the household budgetary needs of his widowed mother. By 1875 William was listed in the Albany City Directory as being employed as a Clerk for the State-Boards. In about 1884, at age twenty-seven, William left the family home and married **Mary A. Curley** at the Sacred Heart Church in Albany. Mary was born in Ireland on February 16, 1860.

William and Mary lived at 28 Center Street in Menands (just over the Albany line; the building is gone now) following their marriage. Together they became parents of six children. A fun question for future researchers is, was our grandfather Dennin's first wife, Mary Curley, related in any way to James Michael Curley (1874-1958), who followed Rose Kennedy's father "Honey Fitz" as a long-term Mayor of Boston?

Of the six children born to William and Mary, **Isabella M.** (born in October 1885), **Edgar** (born in 1889), and **Marion** (born in 1890) all survived to adulthood. **Bessie** (1888 - 1889), **John** (1890 – 1891), and **Martha** (1891-1893) all died in infancy. Mary Curley Dennin died tragically of tuberculosis on July 12, 1893 at the age of thirty-three, in the same year that her youngest child, Martha, died. Her funeral was held at Sacred Heart

Church in Albany. Irish women produced children to the point of exhaustion, and many did not live to see their children to adulthood. Medical expertise was very primitive in 1800's. It wasn't until the 1900's that medical standards became more informed.

William was now a thirty-six-year old widower grieving the loss of his wife and three of his children. Clearly life was challenging as he continued in his job and had to make decisions about how to raise two motherless daughters aged eight and three and a son, aged four.

According to information from Marjie Dennin, the wife of Edgar's grandson David, the decision was made to send the girls to the McAuley Academy in Ausable, Clinton County, a Catholic boarding school in central New York, where the girls would be educated and well-cared for by the nuns. We don't know what year William made the very sad trip (likely by train) from Albany to Ausable to settle his two daughters into their new life at the McAuley Academy. Information from the New York State census shows that Isabella and Marion Dennin were living in the McAuley Academy by 1900. Edgar may have remained with his father or lived for a time with relatives of his mother in Albany as a youth.

***

Margaret Elizabeth O'Sullivan was a young Irish lass when she caught the eye of William W. Dennin. Six years after Mary Curley Dennin's death, the forty-two-year-old widower took Margaret as his bride and step-mother to his three children, on June 28, 1899. They were married at the Sacred Heart Church in Albany. There was a thirteen-year difference in their age. Margaret and William started their lives together at 28 Irving Street, a three-bedroom home built in 1895. This handsome home still stands today. They later lived at 153 Myrtle Avenue and 4 Bleecker Place before moving to 163 Elm Street in 1908 a tree-lined street near the Capitol. I believe these were rented homes and were not owned by William.

Margaret came from comfortable circumstances and was well-dressed and stylish. What I suspect may be her engagement photograph shows a young woman looking intently into the camera. Her hair is softly styled around her sweet face. She wears a string of pearls around her neck and a fur piece adorns her shoulders. Dresses of the era were often of a dark color, high necked, tight at the waist, and the loose-fitting pleated skirt fell to the ankle. A stiff corset was hidden beneath the dress. Heavy soled ankle-high shoes with a patent leather pointed tip would have completed the outfit. Shoes sold for about two dollars a pair. A hat and gloves were always proper, and often a colorful parasol was used to block the warm sun.

Proper gentlemen sported a three-piece suit with a smart bowler or derby hat. The shirt may have had a detachable upstanding or turnover collar. A tie of silk, fashioned to a flat half-bow, was popular at the neck. Facial hair was in style.

Margaret and William soon began their own family with the addition of Anna on April 20, 1900 and **John W.** in 1902.

Margaret Elizabeth Dennin
My Mother

Born at home on the second day of June in 1903, a Tuesday (Tuesday's child is full of grace), **Margaret Elizabeth Dennin** was the third child born to Margaret and William Dennin and was named after her mother. The family had left the Irving Street home and moved to a larger home just a block away at 153 Myrtle Avenue. While expectant mothers at the turn of the century did not give birth in hospitals, it was common for doctors to attend the mother at her home. Ether was available to make the mother comfortable when needed.

Grandfather Dennin supported his large family through various means. During his career, he worked for The Albany Railroad Company, the local Dobler Brewing

Company at the corner of Myrtle Avenue and South Swan Street, and local insurance companies as a cashier or clerk. At the time of his second marriage in 1899, he served in an official capacity as the chief clerk for the State of New York architect's office in Albany.

Though we don't know exactly when Isabella and Marion Dennin left the McCauley Academy, the New York State Census shows that **Marion** was again living with her father, stepmother Margaret, and her half-siblings on Elm Street by 1905. By 1903 **Isabella** had found work with the City of Albany and was also living with her father and stepmother. While at work on January 9th of 1904, Isabella was stricken, possibly with an attack of appendicitis, and died before she could receive proper medical care. She would have been nineteen years old. By 1914 Marion, at age twenty-four, lived at 47 North Pearl Street and was employed as a clerk. She later moved to Elmhurst, Long Island.

***

The turn of the century was an exciting time to be alive. A New York editorialist wrote that the twentieth century began in the United States with "a sense of euphoria and self-satisfaction, a sure feeling that America is the envy of the world." The nation's twenty-sixth president, Teddy Roosevelt, enjoyed enormous popularity due to the "general contentment of the American people." Thriving industry created many jobs for immigrants and others. In 1901 the New York Stock Exchange exceeded two million shares for the first time, and tycoon J. P. Morgan created the U.S. Steel Company, which became the first billion-dollar corporation in the world. In 1903, the Wright Brothers made aviation history with their first flight at Kitty Hawk, North Carolina. Also in 1903, Henry Ford established The Ford Motor Company in Detroit, Michigan and developed the Model T automobile that sold for $850. All of this led to an extremely low unemployment rate and prosperous times. The Gilded Age was in full swing.

The Albany that my mom was born into was a prosperous community of about 100,000 active and involved citizens. In the year of my mother's birth, life expectancy was fifty-two years for females in the United States. Electricity was slowly emerging into American homes. Alexander Graham Bell's telephone, invented in 1876, was now being used in many homes. Horse-drawn carriages were giving way to automobiles. The Union consisted of forty-six states; New Mexico, Arizona, Alaska and Hawaii had yet to be admitted. The average wage was twelve dollars and ninety-eight cents for a fifty-hour work week. Homes were typically heated by coal furnace.

In late December of 1904 **William Wilfred Dennin Jr**. joined older siblings Ann, John and Margaret in this growing family. The fifth child of Margaret and William Dennin, **Rose Mary**, was born in 1907. William and Margaret's sixth and last child, **Joseph**, was born in 1909, the same year that President Taft was elected the twenty-seventh president of the United States. Margaret was thirty-four years of age and William was forty-seven years old. In the first ten years of their marriage, Margaret had given William six children. And they all survived infancy—a rare blessing in those years.

Large families were common in this era. The Dennin family now lived in a comfortable home at 163 Elm Street, the same home in which Margaret's parents, the O'Sullivans, had resided. Brother Don remembers hearing that our grandfather William rented a white Stanley Steamer for Sunday drives in the country.

Young Margaret (my mom, who was now known as Marge) contracted scarlet fever as a child. This was a highly contagious and dangerous disease in the early twentieth century. Aunt Ann's daughter, **Joanne Braun**, wrote to me in a 1988 letter that:

"My mother [Ann] was the only one in the family who had had it [scarlet fever], so she had to take care of Marge. The two of them were quarantined in an upstairs bedroom

for weeks, during which they got their meals through the window by means of a basket on a rope. To amuse your mother and to help pass the time, my mother used to dress up and make up skits in which she played all the parts."

As a result of sisterly attention/inattention, Marge would go through life with a small piece of her right ear lobe missing. It seems that Ann had offered to give Marge a haircut (probably during this period of confinement) and inadvertently snipped off a small part of Marge's ear lobe. Had to hurt just a bit!

A separate incident during Marge's youth brought about extensive and life-long scarring to her upper right underarm area. While attempting to light a candle (possibly on someone's birthday cake), Mom reached across the top of a burning candle. Her blouse sleeve caught fire and left a sizeable and, no doubt, very painful reminder never to get close to fire. There would be a second, even more painful, burn that would come much later in her life.

In the warm summer months, the Dennin children swam in the Normanskill Creek, where they also ice skated in the winter months. The trek from their Elm Street home across Lincoln Park and Morton Avenue to the creek was lengthy. During one ice skating outing, according to Joanne, her mother Ann broke her ankle while skating and *"had to hobble all the way back home to Elm Street."*

In later years, Mom recalled the delightful clippety-clop of horses' hooves on the cobblestone streets of the city as the Normans Kill Dairy milk wagon approached their Elm Street home, or when Tim the ice man passed by crying "ice (or rags) for sale." Brother Don recalls Mom telling of the lamplighter's nightly rounds as he lit the gas street lights. Electric refrigerators were not yet found in most homes. The ice box with a separate freezer area for the ice contained milk, eggs, butter or cheese, meat, and possibly a bottle or two of locally brewed beer.

Mom also told the story of Assemblyman and soon-to-be Governor Al Smith's frequent walks on Elm Street on his way to and from the Capitol building in Albany. He often acknowledged the children while they were at play by patting them on the head or shoulder.

Mom also remembered an earlier Elm Street resident by the name of Parker Dunn, the son of an Albany police officer who had served in The Great War. PFC Dunn died a hero in France less than three weeks before the war ended and was subsequently awarded the Medal of Honor by President Calvin Coolidge. The largest of three Albany bridges over the Hudson was named for Private Parker F. Dunn. The first Dunn Memorial Bridge was dedicated in 1933. It was replaced by the current bridge of the same name in the late 1960s.

***

On April 15, 1912 when Mom was nine years old, the British luxury liner *RMS Titanic* struck an iceberg in the North Atlantic Ocean off Newfoundland on its maiden voyage and sank, killing more than 1,500 people. The United States elected Woodrow Wilson as its twenty-eighth president the following year and on June 28, 1914 Archduke Ferdinand of Austria, the heir to the Austrian-Hungarian Empire, was assassinated which led to the beginning of the First World War. The United States did not immediately join the war, although American cargo ships aided in the war effort by bringing supplies to Europe. German submarines targeted these ships.

On May 7, 1915, the British Cunard ocean liner *Lusitania* was hit by a German sub and sank in eighteen minutes killing 1,198 men, women and children, including 128 Americans.

Isolationism had kept the United States out of the war until April of 1917 when President Woodrow Wilson declared war on Germany to make the world "safe for democracy." Over sixteen million people would die world-wide in The Great War. The war continued until the eleventh hour of the eleventh day of the eleventh month in 1918, when "The War to End all Wars" officially ended with the signing of the armistice known as the Treaty of Versailles.

***

The world was a fast-changing and exciting place as Marge and her five siblings grew up in the early years of the twentieth century. New products, such as electric ranges, vacuum cleaners, radios, electric irons, toasters, and even refrigerators, slowly came on the market—at first only for the wealthy, but were soon available to middle class Americans through something new called the installment plan.

A New York City newspaper article dated May 11, 1916 warned that "*Styles Lure Youths to Their Doom*" and would lead to "*Man's Downfall.*" The story read that "*The deep V-cuts of the new styled 'waists' (*blouses*), the transparent sleeves and shorter skirts were luring young men to their moral doom.*" Oh, the innocence!

***

The Dennin family was a happy one. The children attended The Cathedral School, run by the Sisters of St. Joseph, at 105 Elm Street in Albany. Their father William was remembered as having an excellent singing voice. He was a member of the Albany Light Opera and performed in many of the local Gilbert & Sullivan theater productions in Albany, according to Joanne. He also participated in the choir at the Cathedral. Marge also remembered her father entertaining his family by singing at home. Although these were heady times for the country and the family, tragedy was never far from their doorstep.

***

Exactly one hundred years before this story was written, the deadliest pandemic in modern history took hold. Known as the Spanish flu, the illness made its first impact in the spring of 1918 and was somewhat mild, but it returned in the fall with a vengeance. It swept the world and killed an estimated fifty to seventy-five million people—three percent of the world population. Large numbers of its victims were young, in the prime of their lives and previously healthy people. Many were dead in the course of just a few days or hours with very high fevers as their lungs filled with fluid that caused suffocation. Whole families were gone in two days. Drugs and vaccines were not available to stop the spread of this terror. Schools, theaters, churches, bars, and other gathering places were ordered closed as normal life came to a halt. People were told to wear gauze masks in an attempt to stop the spread of germs. The flu continued into 1919. More than twenty-five percent of the U.S. population became sick and nearly 700,000 Americans died.

One of those victims was my grandfather, William W. Dennin, who died five days before Christmas of 1918 at the age of sixty-one and just a month after World War I ended. William left behind his wife of nineteen years along with their six children (Ann was eighteen; John sixteen; my mother fifteen; Bill fourteen; Rose ten and Joe nine) to support. The two-surviving stepchildren, Edgar and Marion, were by then adults.

An article from the local newspaper at the time of his death tells that William *"was prominent in Democratic circles for many years,"* and that *"the city loses one of its best and highly respected citizens."* The family received visitors at the 163 Elm Street home and the funeral was held the next day at the Cathedral of the Immaculate Conception. One cannot imagine the horror of losing a husband and father so suddenly, combined with the terror of wondering which family member would be the next to die in the plague.

Grandma Dennin was forty-eight years old. How did she manage to support her large family and keep them together to complete their education in the days before pensions or Social Security were available? Ann had graduated and worked as a stenographer for the State by 1920. John also had graduated high school and was employed as a clerk for the State of New York in 1919 and later became a real estate agent. In 1922 they all still lived at the 163 Elm Street home. Possibly there was some financial help from Grandma's brother-in-law Frank P. Dolan, a wealthy local builder, realtor and businessman, who was married to Grandma's sister, Anna.

Grandma's sister Anna O'Sullivan and husband Frank Dolan's marriage produced two children: a son who died in his youth and a daughter, Eileen, born in 1905. Eileen's first marriage to Rensselaer County Judge De Forest Pitt ended in divorce. Eileen then married a military man, Colonel Arthur Scherrer. They later lived at 439 State Street in Albany—a still fashionable block of historic three-story brick and stone homes built in the late 1800's. The interior of their home featured ornate woodwork, oriental carpets, thick red velvet drapes and a magnificent staircase hand-crafted from chestnut. At some point after the Scherrers had left the home, the stairway was reportedly auctioned by Sotheby's for an eye-popping price tag. As a young child visiting the home with my mother, I loved touching the soft velvet of the drapes and remember being fascinated by a dumbwaiter in the house which brought food from the basement kitchen to the dining room. Eileen died in 1971 and had no children from either marriage.

Another relative, Cousin Wilson Sullivan, who was the city editor of the *Albany Times-Union* from 1926 to 1933, and later was the founder and chairman of O'Connor-Sullivan, one of the city's most prominent real estate brokerage firms, may have helped Margaret.

It is likely that Bill and John earned additional money by selling newspapers. Newspaper boys carefully selected and claimed a busy corner and shouted out the headlines of the day as people passed by in the early morning hours. They earned one cent a paper.

Cousin Joe Dennin tells us that his dad (my Uncle

PEG CRIST MCCLOSKEY

Bill) was a classmate of Governor Al Smith's son at the time of William Dennin Sr.'s death. Because the governor knew the family from his walks past their home, he understood the dire financial situation Margaret faced. Bill was only around fourteen years old when the governor offered him a part-time position at the nearby Capitol. Bill did well and later began full-time work at the Capitol following his graduation from The Cathedral School. As time passed, Bill earned a reputation as being a valued employee. When Governor Smith left to run for president in 1928, the incoming governor was Franklin Delano Roosevelt. Joe's family lore is that outgoing Governor Smith asked only one favor of incoming Governor Roosevelt: "Please do not fire Bill Dennin as I couldn't run the Capitol without him." FDR agreed, but the promise was short-lived. As the new administration took hold, young Bill was soon fired by FDR. As he was leaving the building that day, Bill encountered a prominent senator by the name of Jimmy Walker. Walker asked Bill how he was doing and Bill replied "Not so great. I just got fired." Walker immediately hired Bill and eventually wanted Bill to join him in New York City following his election as mayor of the city. Bill would love to have accepted the offer, but to honor his mother who did not want him in the big city, Bill turned down Jimmy Walker's job offer and his career took a very different path.

***

As my mother and her sister Ann neared adulthood, women did not yet have the right to vote. The suffragette movement had begun in July of 1848 just two hundred miles west of Albany in Seneca Falls at the first women's rights convention. Suffragettes Elizabeth Cady Stanton, Lucretia Mott and Susan B. Anthony played prominent roles in the women's movement. A document signed by sixty-eight 'ladies' and thirty-two 'gentlemen' entitled "Declaration of Rights and Sentiments" emerged from the convention and read in part: "*We hold these truths to be self-evident that all men **and women** are created equal.*"

Only one of the original sixty-eight ladies, Charlotte Woodward, lived long enough to see the Nineteenth Amendment ratified.

Forgive me as I very briefly digress from our family story to tell Charlotte's story. And please, as you read her story, remember yourself as a nineteen-year old man or woman. From Hillary Clinton's *What Happened*:

"*In 1848, Charlotte was a nineteen-year-old glove maker living in the small town of Waterloo, New York. She would sit and sew for hours every day, working for meager wages with no hope of ever getting an education or owning property. Charlotte knew that if she married, she, any children she might have, and all her worldly possessions would belong to her husband. She would never be a full and equal citizen, never vote, certainly never run for office. One hot summer day, Charlotte heard about a women's rights conference in a nearby town. She ran from house to house, sharing the news. Some of her friends were as excited as she was. Others were amused or dismissive. A few agreed to go with her to see it for themselves. They left early on the morning of July 19 in a wagon drawn by farm horses. At first, the road was empty, and they wondered if no one else was coming. At the next crossroads, there were wagons and carriages, and then more appeared, all headed to Wesleyan Chapel in Seneca Falls. Charlotte and her friends joined the procession, headed toward a future they could only dream of. Charlotte was more than ninety years old when she finally gained the right to vote, but she got there.*"

Large groups of Albany women were also active in the cause and could often be seen marching to the Capitol to push their case. In 1917 thirty-three suffragists from the National Woman's Party were jailed in Washington, D.C. in vermin-infested cells, beaten, and denied medical help because they dared to picket outside the White House for the right to vote. The struggle for this basic right finally

27

came to an end on August 18, 1920 when the ratification of the 19th amendment finally gave women the right to vote. My mother was seventeen years old.

***

1920 brought other encompassing changes to the population. The Women's Christian Temperance Union and the Anti-Saloon League had fought for and brought about a constitutional ban, which became known as The National Prohibition Act, on production, importation, or manufacture of alcoholic beverages. Prohibition brought about the creation of speakeasy clubs where a secret password was needed to gain entry. One can suspect that young Marge along with siblings Ann, John, and Bill, and their friends, may well have been part of this Roaring Twenties scene while learning the newest dance rage, the Charleston. Flappers were everywhere setting the tone for fun. Prohibition remained in effect until December of 1933 when the ratification of the 21st amendment to the Constitution repealed the 18th amendment, once again legalizing the sale of alcohol. Popular music of the day came from performers such as Bessie Smith, "After You've Gone," Louis Armstrong's "Basin Street Blues," or "April Showers" by Al Jolson. Duke Ellington, Count Basie, and Benny Goodman all were beloved artists of the era.

***

Just two short years after William's death, the Dennin family suffered another tremendous loss. **Rose Dennin** died on January 13, 1920 at the age of thirteen following surgery to remove a cancerous leg. Rose's funeral was at the Cathedral of the Immaculate Conception, as were the funerals of other family members who came before and after her. My mother, at age seventeen, had now endured the sudden loss of her beloved father and a younger sister within two years—both in tragic circumstances. And the Dennin family would endure yet another tragic loss in the not-too-distant future. Marge's youngest brother, **Joseph W. Dennin**, died of rheumatic fever on July 21, 1925 at the age of sixteen.

***

Marge completed high school at The Cathedral School, graduating in 1921. At the Cathedral, she was a popular and proud student, got good grades, and captained the girls' basketball team.

A formal photograph of Marge, likely taken at the time of her high school graduation, seems to reflect the heartbreak she had so recently endured in her young life. Marge's expression in the photo is of a very thoughtful— possibly even sad—young woman. Her dark hair falls well below her slight shoulders in stovepipe curls and one small wispy curl appears on her forehead. She wears a stylish and pretty white graduation dress made of a lightweight fabric, possibly crepe silk. A lavaliere pendant on a chain is around her neck.

The Mildred Elley Secretarial School for Girls was established in 1917. Its advertisements advised young women that "thousands of girls are needed in business and government offices NOW." Upon graduation from The Cathedral School, Marge enrolled in Mildred Elley at 227- 229 Quail Street in Albany. This was a respected local institution which prepared young women for employment in government and private offices. (Some 100 years later, Mildred Elley is still graduating students in more far- flung fields, including technology, and has expanded into other states.) At the time Marge was a student, error-free typing, spelling, grammar, Gregg shorthand and basic bookkeeping skills were taught in the year-long program, along with deportment and a firm instruction to never chew gum while at work or at school.

Following completion of her courses at Mildred Elley, Marge sought nearby employment and by 1925 was employed as a stenographer at the State Capitol. The average annual wage in 1922 was $750. Milk sold for thirty-two cents per gallon. The population of the United States had reached an amazing 100 million people. KDKA in Pittsburgh became the first radio station to offer regular broadcasts.

Marge's five-year high school class reunion was celebrated at The Hampton Hotel on April 3, 1926. Many of her former classmates signed her program—including names we heard remembered many times over the years—Helen O'Meara, Alice Connors, and Letty Donovan among others.

In the next decade, Grandmother Margaret's surviving four children would all set out to establish their adult lives. John and Bill married and began building their careers, while Ann and Marge were busy creating their own families. By 1930 Grandma Dennin had given up her home on Elm Street and was living with son John and his wife Betty at 28A Morris Street. In 1934 the three moved to 6 South Lake Avenue where they remained until John and Betty moved to Rochester.

Patrick and Bridget's legacy produced a large and ever-growing family that continues today in Albany and nearby towns some 150 years after they left Ireland to make a better life.

The Crists

The Crist Family Line

THE CRIST FAMILY LINE

CASPER SHEERER
B: 1795 Germany
D: 1864 Pennsylvania

CHRISTIAN CHRIST
B: 1816 Germany
D: 1893 Pennsylvania

MARGARET SHEERER
B: 1794 Germany
D: 1873 Pennsylvania

MICHAEL ROBERT CRIST
B: 1865 Pennsylvania
D: 1954 Albany, New York

MARGARET SHEERER CHRIST
B: 1826 Germany
D: 1907 Pennsylvania

ROBERT MICHAEL CRIST
B: 1899 Albany, New York
D: 1999 Castleton on Hudson, NY

JOHN BESCH
B: 1820 Germany
D: 1903 Albany, New York

MARY BESCH
B: 1865 Albany, New York
D: 1924 Albany, New York

ROSA KELLER
B: 1826 Germany
D: 1896 Albany, New York

C(K)asper Sheerer
My Paternal Great-great-grandparents (Paternal Side)

Casper Sheerer was born in Burgstall an der Murr, in the state of Baden-Württemberg, Germany in 1795. His wife, **Margaret** (maiden name unknown), was also born in Germany in Bad Mergentheim, Province of Baden-Württemberg in 1794. They became the parents of two sons, Michael and Lebert, and two daughters: Catherine, and **Margaretta** who was born on June 24, 1826 in Linsterlohm, in the Town of Bad Mergentheim, in Baden-Württemberg. There may have been other children, but I have no information on them. Margaret and Casper and daughter Margaret left Germany to escape political unrest in 1845 and immigrated to the United States. Casper died in 1864 in Honesdale, Pennsylvania and Margaret died there on December 23, 1873.

Johan Bösch
My Paternal Great-grandfather (maternal side)

Johan Bösch (later John Besch) was born in June in 1820 in Baden Baden in Baden-Württemberg, Germany. John eventually left Germany, according to the 1892 Census, because he did not believe in the military policies of Germany at the time. John worked as a locksmith and a cabinetmaker and lived in Albany on Delaware Turnpike at Morton Avenue in 1863. In 1878, he lived at 220 Morton Avenue. He was married to Rosa Keller. He died in 1903 at age eighty-three in Albany. [Author's note: When our ancestors left what we now understand to be modern Germany, the area was a collection of individual kingdoms or provinces that were not formed into a country. Therefore, I have chosen throughout to use the modern definition of "Germany" even though the terminology was different at the time of our ancestors.]

Rosa Keller
My Paternal Great-grandmother (Maternal Side)

Rosa Keller was born in Karlsruhe in Baden-Württemberg, Germany in 1826 and immigrated to the United States. Rosa married John Besch and they became parents of twins Amelia and Wilhemina (b. 1855), **Mary** (b. 1865) and five sons (listed below under Mary Besch). Rosa died June 7, 1896 in Albany at seventy years of age.

Christian Christ
My Paternal Great-grandfather (Paternal Side)

Christian H. Christ was born in Bohl, (which is now Rhineland-Palatinate) in Germany on August 10, 1816. On May 20, 1852 at age thirty-six, Christian sailed from Le Havre aboard the vessel *Gertrude* in steerage class en route for New York. He left Germany "in favor of the United States" according to the census. Many German immigrants in the mid-1800s found their way to Pennsylvania and Christian eventually settled in Texas Township near Honesdale, Pennsylvania. He married Casper and **Margaret** Sheerer's daughter Margaret in 1852. (Margaret had a previous husband and they had a son by the name of John Waggand who was born in 1849.) Christian and Margaret became parents to two sons, William (b:1859) and **Michael** (b:1865); and two daughters, Mary (b. 1855,) and Christina (b. 1862 and also called Denair.)

Christian died in Honesdale, Pennsylvania on December 11, 1893 at seventy-seven. The local paper at the time noted: *"It is said that a good name is better than riches. That being the case, Christian Christ who recently died in Wayne County at an advanced age, ought to have fared well during his lifetime."* Margaret died in Honesdale on June 16, 1907 at eighty-one years of age.

Michael Robert Christ (Krist) (Crist)
My Paternal Grandfather (Paternal Side)

Michael Christ, (later Crist) the son of Christian and Margaret Sheerer Christ, was born March 13, 1865 and grew up in Honesdale, Pennsylvania. Michael Crist left Honesdale at a young age to pursue a career as a cigar manufacturer in New York City. He learned the trade from the Ferber Company in Honesdale according to information given by Aunt Kathryn to Uncle Bill Crist's son Bill. (Young Bill wrote me in August of 1984 in response to my inquiries for family history). As a young man, Michael traveled throughout parts of New York State and many of the forty-four existing states as a cigar salesman.

Mary Bösch
My Paternal Grandmother (Maternal Side)

Mary Bösch (later Besch) was born in 1865 in Albany, New York to Johan Bösch and Rosa Keller. Mary had five brothers who would be my great uncles: Frank, listed as a paver in 1883 in the Albany Directory; Henry a businessman who ran an Albany hotel and saloons; (1864-1944), Edward (machinist), John (a brewer) and Joe. As an adult, John left Albany for the gold rush. Joe became a lawyer and had two sons: Clayton (1898-1990) and Joseph, Jr. (1896-1977). Clayton had a son and Joe had twin girls. Henry married two Pappen girls—first Kate who died and then Minnie. Henry was a successful local businessman and served as a deputy sheriff in Albany at the turn of the century. Joseph Besch, Jr. became a "serious developer" in Albany in the '20s.

Again, from William Kennedy's "O Albany!": "*By the time the twentieth century began, Delaware Avenue had been paved and developers were in serious action, men like Jacob Leonard and Joseph Besch. Joseph Besch, Republican sheriff in the early years of this century, took up where Leonard left off and developed along Delaware from Holland Avenue to Besch Avenue. He built the second concrete-block building in Albany . . . People thought they were prisons. Besch also bought three farms and sold lots, creating modern Whitehall Road, previously a muddy wagon path."*

***

The Great Blizzard of 1888 buried Albany and much of the northeast under four feet of snow the year that **Mary Besch** and **Michael Crist** married. Drifts as high as twenty feet covered the city and shut it down for a week, with no services of any type and no food deliveries. Mary and Michael were both twenty-two years old at the time of their marriage and Michael listed his profession as a cigar maker.

While Albany was in the midst of a very large Irish immigration, there also existed a large German immigrant population in the city. Michael and Mary Besch Crist became the parents of eight children between 1889 and 1905: Florence, William, John, Frank, **Robert (my father)**, Edna, Olive and Ethel. More detailed information on each of the children will be found later in the story.

In the late 1800s, Albanians made their way around on trolley cars pulled by one horse or by riding with their own horse attached to a buggy. Michael was a cigar maker from 1889 to 1893 with his business, Crist & Bissi Kummer Cigar Manufacturers, located at 911 Green Street. From 1894 to 1901 Michael worked as a collector for the Hinkel Brewery and lived at 280 Delaware Avenue. In 1904 Michael Crist worked at J & W Bottlers at 171 Jefferson Street while living at 403 Delaware Avenue. He owned or ran several different saloons at various times, including 37 S. Pearl Street in 1907, and was an occasional promoter of enterprise boxing events. Around 1910, Michael purchased and operated the Klondike Hotel at 523 Western Avenue where he would remain for the rest of his life. The Klondike offered rooms and had a stable for guests' horses and at one point had a reputation for being a rough and tumble place.

In 1915, Michael's son John was listed in the City Directory as a carpenter, Will as a painter, Frank as a clerk, and Robert and Edna were listed as students while living at 523 Western Avenue. In 1921 the family lived at 15 Elberon Place. In 1924, the year of Mary Besch Crist's death, the family lived at 295 S. Quail Street. By 1930, Michael had converted the Klondike Hotel into the upscale Marion Apartments where he lived until his death. 523 Western Avenue was a corner lot and also carried the address One North Allen Street.

Like so many of our ancestors, Michael Crist was gifted with a long life. His wife Mary died on February 6, 1924 of colon cancer at age fifty-nine. Michael outlived Mary by thirty years and never remarried. Michael was named honorary Grand Marshal of the German Day parade in Albany just a month before his death in 1954 at eighty-nine. Upon Michael's death on August 9, 1954, a story in the *Albany Knickerbocker News*, written by well-known columnist Charlie Mooney, called Mr. Crist *"a remarkable man who could tell many an interesting story."* Mooney goes on to say that *"tenants of the Marion Apartments say Mr. Crist was a wonderful landlord, and a lot of his friends say he was just as wonderful in other ways."* My recollections of my grandfather are limited. Though I'm sure there were other visits, I remember only one occasion when he visited 2 Benedict Street. He was an elderly man at the time and there was a seventy-six-year age difference between us. There were brief visits over the years to his home on North Allen Street, but I recall very little interaction between us. I remember him as being a somewhat tall and dignified presence. The purpose of most visits would have been for my dad to see his father.

Robert Michael Crist
My Father

Robert Michael Crist was born on March 6, 1899, the fifth child of Michael Crist and Mary Besch Crist. The family lived at 403 Delaware Avenue at the time of Rob's birth. The house is no longer there. Rob later recalled in an Albany *Times Union* article written at the time of his 100th birthday, his home *"had no electricity, no running water, no phone and no radio. It was lit with kerosene lamps and heated by coal stoves in the kitchen and parlor. His parents warmed stones and bottles of water in the oven and placed them under the covers at night."* He went on to say that *"kids had bikes, wagons and played card games. In the winter, you'd go into the root cellar to the apple bin and eat two or three before bed."* His mother's sauerbraten and potato pancakes were favorites at the dinner table.

Rob's childhood was not unlike that of Marge Dennin's, as she was growing up just a few miles away. Both came from large families, although Rob's heritage was entirely of German descent, while Marge was all Irish. And like Marge, Rob would lose a parent in his early adulthood. Neither family was wealthy by modern standards; however, each maintained a solid middle-class lifestyle. The children were all educated and seemed to thrive.

Like the young Dennins, Rob and his siblings enjoyed swimming, skating, and fishing at Normanskill Creek. A photo appearing in the local newspaper shows Rob at perhaps age eleven or twelve holding a large fish he had caught. He wears knickers, the classic look of the era for boys. Neighborhood baseball pick-up games were also a very popular activity for Rob and his friends while he was young.

Albany High School opened the doors to a glorious new building in 1914. The large two-story ornate masonry building was fronted on one end with columns

37

in Greco-Roman style. The school was located on Lake Street between Washington and Western Avenues. Nephew Craig remembered Pops telling him that, with so many men away at war in 1917-18, his class at Albany High School was sent to work at nearby farms during their senior year to help the war effort. Brother Jack recalls Dad saying that he had been a member of the first graduating class of the new school.

On the 5th day of June 1917, when my father was eighteen years old, a new law known as The Selective Service Act was enacted. It required all men between the ages of twenty-one and thirty to register for military service. My father's three older brothers, ages twenty-six, twenty-four, and twenty-one, complied with the law and ultimately served their country during the war years.

A year later the law was revised to require men who had "attained the age of 21 after June 5, 1917" to register for the draft. And lastly, on September 12, 1918 the Draft Board required all young men between the age of eighteen and forty-five to register for the draft. A copy of my father's draft registration shows that he registered on September 12, 1918 and indicated that his occupation was "student at Albany High School." The war ended a little more than a month later.

Craig once asked my father why he hadn't served in the Great War. Pops told Craig that, as the youngest son in his family, he felt great pressure from his mother and father to stay home from the war. His three older brothers were serving and that was enough sacrifice for any family to make.

Brother Dick suggested that the army would not take a fourth son. Knowing my father's personality, I have no doubt that he felt remorseful in not joining his brothers in the war effort. One also wonders if Dad and other members of his family suffered any discrimination as second-generation Germans at the time of the First World War or in succeeding years.

Six of our family's uncles: William, John and Frank

Crist, Edmund Braun, Raymond Joyce Sr., and Dr. Charles Perry, served their country during the Great War. Their stories are detailed later.

On November 23, 1921 at age twenty-two, Rob enlisted in Troop B of the First Cavalry of the New York State Guard. Troop B was assigned to the New Scotland Avenue Armory and was somewhat akin to the present-day National Guard. As a member of the Cavalry, Rob was assigned a horse. Dad always spoke fondly of his horse who was named Bugler.

***

Dad began working as a junior clerk for the New York State Health Department in about 1919. His starting salary was $600 per year. In 1923 he became a multigraph operator and later that year a motion picture operator. In 1925 he lived at 738 Myrtle Avenue. In 1926 he lived at 264 Partridge Street. In 1928 Dad became a supervisor of visual instruction at the New York State Health Department Film Library in the Capitol.

Dad's brother Frank also worked for the New York State Health Department Film Library and, as part of their duties, the two brothers took the occasional road trip to western parts of the state such as Geneseo, south of Rochester. They also visited Port Leyden, and Utica, among other cities, while bringing along and showing public health films in different venues, including the state fair in Syracuse. They traveled and slept in the State "Healthmobile".

An article from the November 4, 1924 edition of the Wyoming County Times, Warsaw, N.Y. describes a close call for Rob and his co-worker and friend, Ben Minch:

"The *State Healthmobile which has been in Livingston County for the past two weeks giving a series of health pictures caught fire last Wednesday evening.*" The article goes on to say, "*the engine stalled and in endeavoring to start it flames burst from under the gas tank located in the cab. Benjamin Minch and **Robert Crist** from Albany, who* *were in charge of the car, leaped from the cab as the flames burst through. They made an attempt to put out the fire with a hand extinguisher, but to no avail. Seeing that this was useless they successfully removed the picture machine and films from the rear of the truck."*

***

Also employed at the New York State Health Department in the Capitol was Marge Dennin. The Capitol was only about twenty years old at the time and was the most expensive building in the country, having cost an outrageous twenty-five million dollars to build. It was there that Marge and Rob got to know each other and learned of their similar backgrounds in Albany. Marge and Rob began a courtship, which included lunch-time mandolin strumming and singing on the rooftop of the Capitol Building and weekend riding in the countryside. As an active member of Troop B, Rob was permitted to bring his favorite date, Marge Dennin, for occasional recreational weekend rides with the Troop B horses. Both became excellent riders and enjoyed this time together.

Marge discovered that Rob was also a bit of a composer. During the period of World War I, patriotic fervor was rampant. Rob had written and copyrighted the lyrics for a new song, "*When the War Is Over*" in 1918. The music was written by E.S.S. Huntington who was a prolific composer at the time with many copyrights to his/her credit. Rob lived at 523 Western Avenue in Albany at the time of the copyright.

From brother Jack we learn that members of Troop B kept and rode their horses on a large piece of rural property near Nassau and Chatham, outside of Albany. Years later, Jack and Lynne bought a home built on a parcel of the very same property. Dad told Jack that he and Mom had ridden their horses on this same land when he was a member of Troop B.

Marge and Rob became part of a group of friends called the Tillicums. Tillicum was a Chinook Indian word which meant "friend." These friends had great times together at a nearby camp at Thompson Lake and were remembered fondly throughout the years.

At some point, likely in 1927, Rob and Marge became engaged when Rob presented her with a stunning one-half carat diamond solitaire set in platinum and asked her to be his bride. While not so remarkable in today's world, the ring was quite extravagant for the twenties. And so began a lifetime together that would endure for more than forty years.

Part Two

The Early Years

I Do

On Wednesday, August 1, 1928, Margaret Elizabeth Dennin was married to Robert Michael Crist. At just five feet tall, Marge was a very pretty and petite young woman with dark hair and brilliant blue eyes. Her formal bridal portrait depicts a shy smile in a classic pose. She wears a delicate white dress with a loose fitting, below-the-knee hemline. The dress is sleeveless with a jewel neckline and displays a small decorative pearl-encrusted applique on the right hip area. White gloves reach her elbow. A soft white hat with a large brim frames her face and anchors her hem length veil. Her hair is styled with smooth waves around her face in a classic 20s look and is cut just below the ear. Earrings are not visible. Around her neck on a chain, is the same lavaliere that was seen in her graduation photo years earlier. I believe the lavaliere was a family piece, possibly belonging to her mother. The lavaliere is sadly lost to history.

To my knowledge there are no surviving photos of Marge and Rob together on their wedding day. However, other contemporary pictures show Rob as a dashing figure. He was a young man, trim at about five feet ten inches, who had done well thus far in life and expected to do even better in the future. His dark hair was parted in the middle as was the fashion for men at the time. He sported a thin pencil mustache which he maintained throughout much of his life. He had a great interest in the thriving 1920s stock market and had made investments that helped to finance their wedding, including Marge's diamond, their new home, and their new 1928 Chevrolet purchased for $615. In 1916, there were only four million cars on the road in the U.S. By

1928, cars had become a normalcy for middle-class buyers with twenty-four million cars on the road.

Although Marge was a faithful Catholic and an active member of the Parish of the Cathedral of the Immaculate Conception on Eagle Street, where her mother attended daily mass, she was not permitted by the church to be married at the main altar of the Cathedral because Rob was a protestant. Instead, Rob and Marge were married in Saint Anne's Chapel, which is a separate area to the left of the main altar. This area is presently used as the sacristy. A fireplace fills one corner of this room and we have been told the bride and groom would have stood before the fireplace as they took their vows before the Reverend J. A. Delaney. They were a handsome couple. Marge was twenty-five and Rob was twenty-nine. Marge's sister, Ann, and Rob's brother, John, served as their attendants.

They had no idea that the happiness they shared on their wedding day would be shaken by terrible storm clouds which awaited them, and which would strike again and again throughout their married life.

Family Beginnings

Rob and Marge traveled to Cape Cod and New England for their honeymoon. Marge sent her mother a letter from Cambridge, Massachusetts where they visited both Harvard and MIT, along with the usual tourist stops in Boston. From there they drove through Revere Beach, Lynn, Marblehead, Salem, Gloucester and Hampton Beach where they stayed for three days at The Garland. *"Boy, it was so hot we didn't even feel like moving. We just put on our bathing suits and stayed in the ocean. Old Sol just poured down on that beach until you could cook eggs in the sand. Bob and I are pretty much sunburned and believe me it is sore."* I remember Mom saying that when their feet hit the sand that day, it was so hot that they had to dash frantically for the water.

It was Mom's (and maybe Dad's) first look at an ocean. *"I am crazy about the ocean. When you look out, all you can see is sea and sky, and you can't tell where one leaves off and another begins."* From Hampton Beach they drove north to Old Orchard Beach in Maine where they stayed at the Hotel Vesper and the weather was cooler. In her third letter home, dated August 6, 1928, Mom expressed her loneliness for the family, *"I'd give a lot if I could hear from home. I get the homesick blues every once in a while."* After an overnight in Portland, they made their way back to begin their new life together in Albany.

Following their honeymoon, Marge and Rob set up housekeeping in their brand-new two-bedroom 1300 sq. ft. house at 66 Cardinal Avenue in Albany. They were off to a great start. Marge was now a stay-at-home housewife, having left her job with the Health Department as was the practice of most brides of the era.

Early in their marriage—I suspect on their first anniversary—Marge and Rob traveled to Canada where they stayed at the famed Château Frontenac in Quebec City. Prohibition was still the law of the land in the U.S., unlike in Canada where liquor purchases were legal. Jack remembers hearing that *"Rob and Marge had made some liquor purchases while in Canada. Coming back through the border, cars were stopped and searched. The agents, it turns out, never thought to look under the hood where Rob had hidden his stash of Canadian liquor."* Score one for Dad's American ingenuity.

What no one could know was that "Black Tuesday" along with the complete collapse of stock market prices, would arrive on October 29, 1929 and was followed by The Great Depression—just slightly more than a year after Rob and Marge were married. Billions of 1929 dollars were lost in the previously booming stock market, banks failed, and savings were wiped out as people struggled to survive. Because stocks could be bought "on margin," meaning the buyer had to put up only ten percent of the purchase price, when the markets failed people were liable for the full price of the stock.

Rob was employed by the State Health Department which meant his job was secure, but substantial pay cuts were the norm for those fortunate enough to have a job in a world with a twenty-five percent unemployment rate. It would be ten years before the economy returned to a healthy state. I never heard Mom and Dad talk about how they may have suffered during the Great Depression. Like so many others, they learned to live as frugally as possible.

***

For Rob and Marge, life continued at 66 Cardinal Avenue where they were thrilled to welcome baby **Robert Michael Crist, Jr**. on February 7, 1931 born at The Brady Maternity Home on 40 North Main Avenue. Marge loved being a new mother and was known to iron little Bobby's cloth diapers. Bobby was often placed on the large front porch in his carriage for napping in the fresh air. A booklet of ninety-four pages, "Our Babies – Their Feeding, Care and Training" was given by the hospital to the new mom and provided thorough instructions on how to give the baby cod-liver oil the year round and how to wash baby's scalp with kerosene in the event of head lice, among other vital information.

As Bobby grew to be a toddler, he developed a full head of very curly hair, and as a result, happened to bear a remarkable likeness to another well-known baby of about the same age, Charles Lindbergh III. On March 1, 1932 the nineteen-month-old son of aviation hero Charles Lindbergh II, who had flown the first solo flight across the Atlantic Ocean in 1927, was kidnapped from his bedroom in Hopewell, New Jersey. The story, with large pictures of baby Lindbergh, made headlines across the world.

By now, at about fourteen months old, Bobby had left his carriage behind and enjoyed playing with his toys on the porch. Marge soon noticed that people walking past would stop and stare at young Bobby. It wasn't long before Rob and Marge understood that the passersby were wondering if young Bobby was in fact the kidnapped Charles Lindbergh III. Tragically, on May 12, the body of the Lindbergh baby was discovered in a wooded area not far from the Lindbergh home. Federal agencies at the highest levels of government investigated this horrific event and ultimately charged a German immigrant by the name of Bruno Hauptmann with the crimes of kidnapping and murder. He was put to death on April 3, 1936.

***

It wasn't long before Mom and Dad were setting up a second nursery in their home. At fifteen months old, Bobby welcomed his new baby brother to the family. **John Joseph Crist**, was born on August 23, 1932 and joined the family at 66 Cardinal Avenue. Jack still has the paid receipt for his birth at The Brady Maternity Home in Albany, including a nine-day hospital stay at four dollars per day for his mom. Total charges were forty-three dollars.

***

An event even more ominous than the Great Depression was about to engulf Rob and Marge and their young sons. In the late fall of 1932, my father was diagnosed with tuberculosis and became a patient at a sanitarium in Saranac Lake, New York.

Consumption—also known as "the white plague" and more commonly as tuberculosis—is an ancient disease and has been traced back thousands of years to the earliest civilizations; from 1500 BC India and early Chinese dynasties to the Persian Empire to pre-Columbian America to Europe in the Middle Ages and Renaissance to the New World. Many bizarre treatments were devised over the millennia, but few, if any, brought about a certain cure. It is a bacterial disease, usually affecting the lungs, and is spread mostly in the air from person to person. And it killed many of its victims. In the mid-1800s a new treatment plan was devised. Patients were to be sent to a sanitarium where they would be made to rest, breathe fresh mountain air, and eat a diet heavy in protein to counterattack the tuberculosis bacterium.

The Adirondack Cottage Sanitarium at Saranac Lake, New York was founded in 1884 by Dr. Edward Livingston Trudeau, himself a former tuberculosis patient. Dr. Trudeau is the great grandfather of "Doonesbury" cartoonist, Gary Trudeau. It continued in service until 1954 when effective antibiotic treatments for tuberculosis were developed. A second sanitarium, The New York State Hospital for Incipient Pulmonary Tuberculosis at near-by Ray Brook, was opened in 1904 and continued to operate until the mid-1960s. Once diagnosed with tuberculosis, patients were often ordered by their local health department to report to a sanitarium within twenty-four hours to prevent spreading the disease to family members. We have been told by Michele Tucker, the historian at the Saranac Lake Library, that because Ray Brook was a state hospital, it is very likely that Rob (a state employee) would have been sent there for his cure.

These sanitaria, or "cure cottages" as some were called, were also known as waiting rooms for death. A devastating diagnosis, tuberculosis was the leading cause of death in the early 1900s. The survival rate for tuberculosis patients in the early 1900s was shockingly low at around fifty percent and varied depending on the stage of the illness and other factors such as age, race, and gender.

Patients were not permitted to see their families up close. I have found no one who remembers Pops sharing any information about being stricken with TB other than Heidi, who remembers Pops telling her that when he had visitors, he was wheeled to the porch of the sanitarium and was allowed only to wave at his family from the porch.

Treatment consisted of resting, eating lots of protein, and being wheeled outside each day to take in the fresh cold, clear mountain air, even during the winter months. In some cases, lungs were collapsed to bring about a cure.

The daily regimen for patients in one sanitarium consisted of the following:

- 7:15 Rising bell
- 8:00 to 8:30 Breakfast
- 8:30 to 11:00 Rest or exercise as ordered
- 11:00 to 12:45 Rest on bed
- 1:00 to 1:30 Dinner
- 1:45 to 4:00 Rest on bed, reading but no talking allowed. Quiet hour.
- 4:00 to 5:45 Rest or exercise as ordered
- 6:00 Supper
- 8:00 Nourishment if ordered
- 9:00 All patients in pavilions
- 9:30 All lights out

Records painstakingly obtained by Nephew Craig Crist from the New York State Local Retirement System show that my father was granted six months leave with pay between September 1, 1932 and March of 1933. We believe this was the period that my father was confined with tuberculosis. Remember that Jack was born in late August of 1932. We don't know the exact dates of my father's confinement as many patient records from Saranac Lake sanitaria were lost to fire or other destruction over the years. But during his months in Saranac Lake, he achieved what many did not—a cure, and was able to return to his family at 66 Cardinal Avenue in early 1933.

None of my siblings or I knew that our father had had TB until well into our adult years. Dad never talked about this experience of having a very serious illness or about his time in the sanitarium as we children grew up. He certainly never complained about it.

I must add that like my father, my mother never talked about this extremely dark and terrifying period in their lives. And, like my father, she never complained. When Dad was stricken, it had been only a few years since Mom had lost her father, sister and brother to sudden fatal illnesses; and now she faced the very real possibility of losing her husband and the father of her very young children to yet another unimaginable death. Dad was thirty-three years old, in the fourth year of his marriage, the father of a sixteen-month old toddler (brother Bob) and a newborn infant (brother Jack). A great Depression raged throughout the world with no way to know if and when it would end. And no way to know if he would ever come home. (A pause here to contemplate the last four sentences).

***

1933 was also the year that Governor Franklin Delano Roosevelt moved on from the State Capitol in Albany following the defeat President Herbert Hoover. FDR become the thirty-second president of the United States and would be the only one ever to be elected four times. The Depression still raged and, in his inaugural address, FDR advised the American people that, *"The only thing we have to fear is fear itself."* His unforgettable remarks reenergized the country. With radios now found in many homes, FDR's famous "fireside chats" continued regularly and served to provide leadership and promote calm among the population.

***

By now Bobby was an active toddler and Jack kept right up with him. The two brothers grew together, rode their trikes on the sidewalks where they were sometimes joined by their cousins, Joanne Braun and Bill Dennin, and had an idyllic childhood. During Bobby's early days of playing on the front porch, another infamous Crist incident occurred. As a marketing tool, manufacturers were known to distribute samples of their products directly to families. One day, a delivery person tossed a packet of "bluing" onto the porch at 66 Cardinal Avenue. Bluing was used to aid in whitening laundry during washing. Unfortunately, Bobby spotted the bluing packet before Mom knew it was there and decided it would taste good. It created quite a fright for Marge to find her baby turning blue, but after discovering what had happened, Bobby recovered quite nicely. Not so sure about his mom.

It was during this period in 1934 and 1935 that Rob enjoyed his hobby of participating in the Albany Field Trials. The purpose of the field trials was to train cocker spaniels to retrieve pheasants after the hunters had brought them down. Rob's silky haired black spaniel, named Robinhurst Gunman, won several awards. Rob filmed many of the field trials with the new color film. The family owned a cocker spaniel by the name of Chummy in later years.

The Move to Castleton

Marge had begun to worry that their wonderful home was no longer a safe place for her children. When Rob and Marge set up housekeeping on Cardinal Avenue, it was a quiet, dead-end street. Unfortunately, city officials later determined that Cardinal Avenue should become a through corridor. Cardinal Avenue was extended to intersect with the adjoining Hackett Boulevard and thus became a busy thoroughfare. It wasn't long before city buses were transiting in front of the no-longer-quiet front yard of 66 Cardinal Avenue. Marge was very concerned that one of her boys could run in front of a car or bus.

Additionally, by early 1936, she was expecting again. With the worries about traffic, and because their home wasn't large enough to accommodate their rapidly expanding family, Marge and Rob made the decision to leave their beloved home behind and move to larger and safer quarters. Rob's brother John was a builder and owned five houses on Allendorf Hill in the nearby peaceful village of Castleton-on-the-Hudson.

Castleton is located nine miles south of Albany on the east bank of the Hudson River. In 1936 it was a prosperous village where most everyone was employed—either locally at the Fort Orange Paper Company (where the daily four o'clock whistle signaled to the entire village that the work day had ended); the Anticorrosive Metal Products which manufactured rust-free parts for war-time engines; or in the City of Albany or the Village of Castleton. Another large employer of locals was The General Aniline and Film (GAF), a nearby German-owned company which was taken over by the government during the war years. Jack remembers Mom telling him that Bayer Aspirin had been invented on their premises. It later became Sterling Winthrop.

Elm trees lined the three-block stretch of Main Street. The thriving area contained, among other establishments, four churches: The Congregational Church at the base of Seaman Avenue, The Dutch Reformed Church, St. Paul's Methodist Church, and St. Giles Episcopal Church. Sacred Heart Catholic Church and the Lutheran Church were located uptown. Four grocery stores on Main Street—The A&P, Sancomb's Meat Market and Grocery, Walt Gersch's IGA, and a Grand Union—kept the population from starving. Garry Roozeboom's hardware store carried a great selection of household necessities. Two drug stores—Sloan's and Rappold's, further down the street—kept folks healthy, and three gas stations with garages: Ulmer's, Lansing's (later Mutterer's), and Carly Heeder's, kept the cars running. There were also Schlosser's jewelry shop; an insurance agency, a tailor shop owned by Fred Frank; and Goodlow's shoe repair shop. At Kilmer's Newsroom you could buy cigarettes, magazines, newspapers, and greeting cards; choose from a delectable array of penny candies, or enjoy some terrific Sealtest ice cream sundaes. I would here work part-time during my senior year in high school and my year at Mildred Elley. My salary was fifty cents per hour.

A movie theater housed in the International Order of Odd Fellows (I.O.O.F.) building kept the kids happy for hours on end on a Saturday afternoon, and men could have their hair styled into a crew cut at George Janke's Barber Shop. In addition, there were at least three businesses where one could have a beer and play some darts: The American House, owned by Patrick McGivern; Clinton's Grill; and The Village Inn. Garafalo's bar and restaurant had yet to open but when it opened in the early 50s, it would become a hugely popular teen-age gathering spot for eating Vera Garafalo's amazing pizza and dancing to juke box favorites. Frank Sinatra's "Witchcraft" was a big favorite while Johnny Mathis's "Misty" always brought the crowd racing to the dance floor.

A post office, the Castleton Bank (which advertised capital of $50,000 and surplus of $50,000) and lastly, the railroad station on Main Street rounded out the necessities of mid-century living. The railroad station was well utilized by passengers traveling to Albany, New York City, or other cities on the eastern seaboard. In the mid-twenties and later, as many as twenty trains a day traveled through Castleton though not all made stops.

Seaman, Scott, Green and Stimpson Avenues each traveled from Main Street uphill to the residential areas of the village where the Catholic and Lutheran churches were located as well as the school which was built in 1923. At one point in the village's earlier history, the A. C. Cheney Piano Action Company prospered on Green Avenue.

The population of the village at the time was about 1,500 people. The Depression still lingered in 1936 even though unemployment rates were down to sixteen percent. The average cost of a house was $3,925. King

Edward VIII abdicated the throne of England to marry his love, commoner and American divorcee, Wallace Simpson; while in Germany an American Black man, Jesse Owens, won four gold medals at the Berlin Olympics, bringing humiliation to Adolph Hitler. Hitler, along with Italy's Benito Mussolini and Japan's Emperor Hirohito, had formed a dangerous alliance—an ominous sign of trouble ahead.

***

In mid-1936 Rob and Marge made the big move to the home on Allendorf Hill in Castleton. They rented from Rob's brother, John. It was a generously-sized and well-built wood-frame shingled home which had a large kitchen, dining room, den and a living room with a brick fireplace on the main level. The upstairs contained four bedrooms and the bathroom. Spacious porches graced the side and front of the house with a glorious view of the river discovered in 1609 by Henry Hudson aboard his ship the *Half Moon*. (Hudson disappeared two years later following a mutiny on a subsequent voyage under the English flag.)

A garage and swings completed the scene outside. As wonderful as the house was, there was a big downside— the narrow, twisty, and steep dirt road on which it was located made it difficult, if not impossible, to access or leave the house by car during wintry weather.

Just a few months after the move to Allendorf Hill, on October 10, 1936, **Richard Allan** Crist entered the world followed seven minutes later by his fraternal twin, **Donald Bruce Crist**. The twins, though premature, were healthy and soon were thriving. Along with two active toddlers, Mom's work was cut out for her. A local woman, Tilly Van Buren, was able to lend a hand with caring for Mom's busy family. The family settled into their new home, the twins grew, and time passed.

Jack recalls that one of his and Bob's playmates was Sally Latham, the daughter of Cal Latham and his wife.

Cal and his brother William ran the local Fort Orange Paper Company, a manufacturing plant which was a large employer of village residents, and which operated twenty-four hours a day during the war, providing plenty of jobs. The Lathams lived in the house just down the hill from Marge and Rob's home. Sally appears in old 16 mm family films famously known as "The Bobby and Jackie Movies." Pops was quite the filmmaker at the time and was able to create amazing events on the screen such as when Mom waved her arm in front of an undecorated Christmas tree which magically became beautifully decorated, and children's legs could mysteriously walk away from their bodies. The Jaros family eventually bought the Latham home and became long-time neighbors.

***

Jack remembers that on New Year's Eve 1936, Rob and Marge hosted a small family get-together to celebrate the New Year with some of Dad's brothers and their wives.

New Year's Day 1937 in Castleton was a brilliant day with a high temperature of forty-five degrees and no precipitation. Dad joined some friends at the local skating pond for an outing. The pond lay tucked off the base of Seaman Avenue at the bottom of Allendorf Hill and was owned by John Amsler, a local businessman who cut blocks of ice from the river and sold them to residents who did not yet have electric refrigerators or to local businesses.

The game Dad and his friends played on ice was called Crack the Whip, a handholding, in-line skating game where the group skated rapidly in a circular pattern. Rob was the last in line, and therefore had to skate faster than everyone else. When he fell, he knew immediately he had a terrible problem. His hip was broken.

There was no local ambulance company, no public phone nearby, and it was a holiday. Jack recalls hearing that somehow Dad managed to get himself up the long steep hill back home—with a broken hip. Ultimately, he was taken to the hospital in Albany where, at age thirty-seven and as the father of four, he was placed in a full body cast from his armpits to below the knee. Just four short years after his recovery from tuberculosis.

Mom now faced each day as the mother of two active youngsters aged six and four, and premature twin boys about three months old, with a husband in a full body cast, in pain and needing time-consuming nursing care. They lived in a house that could become inaccessible in winter weather. Through the grace of God, the winter of 1937 proved to be mild with no major snowfalls to add to the misery.

While Dad healed over the course of many months, Mom continued with her life as well as she could. Tilly Van Buren was still available to help the family and it was likely that some of Dad's family members and Mom's sister, Ann, helped. They all lived in nearby Albany or Delmar and had cars to make the ten-mile trip to Castleton. It is possible that Grandma Dennin moved in for a while to help. There were also neighbors nearby to lend a hand when they could. Mom's brothers Bill and John had moved on from the area to seek their fortunes. Given the unimaginable challenges that Mom faced, she nevertheless survived—without losing her sanity—and eventually nursed Dad back to health after many months. Not an easy task and we can only speculate on the mental toll it all took on Mom.

Dad's job with the State of New York was, once again, secure during his recovery and was waiting upon his return. After having begun his career in the mail room, Dad was named the exhibits supervisor and ultimately became the director of the Film Library of the State of New York Health Department. In this role, Rob oversaw development and distribution of public health films and was a pioneer in the use of color film. Surely this job security was a lifesaver and helped them prevail over the third catastrophic event in eight years of married life.

2 Benedict Street

As the long, dismal winter of 1936-37 slowly came to a close, another much more winter-accessible home became available just up the hill. Benedict Street and Allendorf Hill were one contiguous street, but the name changed at the top of the hill. Like the house on Allendorf Hill, the Benedict Street home had a marvelous sweeping screened-in side porch with expansive views of the Hudson River and a large unscreened front porch with broad steps leading to the lawn. The wide plank, wooden porch floorboards were painted mariner blue while the ceiling consisted of wooden bead boards stained a medium brown color. The wooden railings were painted a rich deep red color. The views of the river were spectacular and provided the perfect spot to watch the beautiful Hudson River Day Line steam ships such as the *Alexander Hamilton*, a side-paddle steamer, the *Robert Fulton* or the *Hendrik Hudson*, pass on the river. The *Peter Stuyvesant* was the last of the great boats to be built. The steam ships' last run came in 1948.

The two-story house, shingled in red cedar, sat toward the end of a long, level unpaved one-lane road on an acre and a third of mostly level land where there was plenty of open space for the kids to run and play safely. Equally important, there was ample space for Rob to cultivate gardens.

However, at 1,100 square feet, the house itself was considerably smaller than the Allendorf Hill home. When built in 1875 the house at 2 Benedict Street originally served as a carriage house for the much larger "manor" home just down at the end of Benedict Street.

In late 1937 the move was made from the Allendorf Hill home up the hill to 2 Benedict Street, which at the time was interestingly also known as 7 Seaman Avenue. Dad still rented from his brother John and later bought this home, along with a second nearby property. The Wodtke family moved to the Allendorf Hill home and sometime later Harold and Marjorie Bailey and their three children moved into that home. The Baileys and their children—Allen, Wayne and Laurel (Lu)—became life-long family friends. And to this day, I still receive a Christmas card each year from my classmate and friend, Gail Wodtke.

In comparison to the Allendorf Hill home, the kitchen at 2 Benedict was much smaller. Approximately ten by ten and a half feet, it had three doors (to the dining room, the spare room and the outside) which consumed much of the available wall space. The room contained a refrigerator, range/oven, and the obligatory kitchen sink with an attached drain board. A three-shelf built-in open cupboard over the sink reached to the ceiling and was the width of the sink and drain board or about four and a half feet wide. A two-shelf unit on wheels served as storage for larger items such as a toaster or deep fryer and stood adjacent to the drain board of the sink. Mom added a sixty-inch high, two-door white metal cabinet to store canned and boxed foods, and a smaller cabinet with one drawer and storage area beneath sat between it and the range. A third waist-high unit about thirty-six inches wide contained two silverware drawers and space underneath to store pots, pans and other cooking utensils. It abutted the refrigerator. The cabinet's Formica top provided counter space for the stand Mixmaster and was the only space in the kitchen available for food preparation. A step stool with a small seat stood near the sink and provided access to the top shelf of the cupboard which held plates, glasses, and food items. A double-hung sash window behind the two-shelf unit overlooked the back yard. The floor was linoleum. A one-bulb ceiling fixture with a string pull cord provided the light.

A breakfast room, or "spare room" as it came to be called, was adjacent laterally to the kitchen and was entered through the kitchen or from the dining room. This room was approximately ten by twelve feet, had one sash window looking out to the back yard, and three doors which accessed the kitchen, the dining room, and the screen porch. The room had no closet.

The spare room served a variety of uses over the years, from toy room to "junk room," to my bedroom, to den, and ultimately in later years became Pops' favorite room where he sat by the window in his green Morris chair and soaked up the warm southern-facing afternoon winter sun. The room also contained Pops' desk and the automatic washing machine in his later years.

The dining room was entered from the kitchen or the spare room, and it in turn was beside the living room. Both rooms had sash windows which opened onto the screen porch. The living room had two additional windows on the wall facing the front lawn and straddled the dark wood and glass double front door. The two rooms abutted with a rectangular archway dividing the space. Both rooms were decorated in Wedgewood blue— the dining room with paint on the plaster walls and the living room walls with wallpaper. The extensive woodwork (surrounding the windows, the many doors, the stairway balusters, the archway and baseboard throughout) was painted crisp white.

A hard-rock maple table stained a medium reddish-brown, along with six matching chairs, dominated the dining room. Leaves at both ends of the table were easily opened to provide more seating space. A matching hutch displayed Mom's English bone china tea cups and plates, and housed her Noritake china and silver serving dishes, while a family heirloom silver tea service sat on the matching buffet. An oval braided early-American style rug covered the floor. The flooring throughout the main level was honey-colored hardwood, with the exception of the kitchen and bathroom.

The lone family bathroom was entered from a third door in the dining room near the kitchen. A fourth door in the dining room provided access to a wooden stairway leading to the basement. A coal furnace and kerosene-fueled hot water heater were found there along with Dad's work bench. A large coal bin stood in the back corner near the furnace and beneath a small window.

The family sofa sat alongside the stairway wall in the living room and several comfortable chairs rounded out the furniture. A dark rose-colored heavy wool carpet covered much of the living room floor. A small table beside the couch provided space for the black rotary dial phone with a corded handset that sat in the cradle of the phone. The cord on the phone was long enough to enable the handset to be carried to the top step of the basement stairway where the door could be closed for some much-needed teenage privacy.

In the center of the floor under the archway between the rooms was the metal grate—known evermore as The Register—which was the only source of heat for the entire house from the coal furnace below in the basement.

A hardwood stairway led from the living room to two bedrooms on the second floor. A hard-rock maple, milled newel post with large rounded finial supported the banister which survived years of the five kids sliding down the banister. A matching post and finial stood at the top of the stairway.

Each upstairs bedroom contained a small sash window on the smaller wall and a large rectangular window on the longer wall facing the river. The larger window was maybe forty-six inches wide by thirty inches high and was opened by lifting it into the room and affixing an arm which kept the window supported. These windows offered great vantage points for viewing the river. Of course there was no air conditioning, so the breezes that came in through those big windows were heavenly on a hot and humid summer night. Each bedroom had a closet tucked under the slanted ceiling of the eave. The upstairs bedroom floors were covered with linoleum and small rugs.

A third bedroom was located on the main level at the bottom of the stairway just off the living room. It contained a closet and two windows; one looking out at the front lawn and one facing the driveway.

The one and only bathroom was just large enough to contain a white claw foot tub, toilet, and sink. There was no shower and there was just enough room for one person to stand before the sink. A medicine cabinet hung over the sink and provided the only mirror. The sash window looked out at the space between the bathroom and the exterior wall of the downstairs bedroom. In the early 50s the claw foot tub was removed, along with the toilet and sink. They were replaced with the very latest in bathroom styling at the time—PINK fixtures, including the tub, toilet and sink. We were all quite thrilled for the first few years, until pink went rapidly out of style. But we now had a shower for the first time ever. The shower head was rigged over the tub and a plastic shower curtain surrounded the tub in a not-always-successful effort to keep the water off the floor.

The house at 2 Benedict had no fireplace and no garage as the Allendorf Hill house had. But the setting was very pretty and the level, open-space land, making the house accessible year-round, made all the difference.

Two chicken coops in the back yard completed the outside of the property and set the stage for a steady supply of eggs, along with the occasional Sunday chicken dinner. It wasn't long before the chicken coops were populated with chickens. The children took turns feeding them and gathering the eggs on a daily basis.

After Dad was fully healed from his broken hip and back at work, he set about establishing a very large garden area in his free time. His garden in later years had a reputation as being one of the best in the village. Plants included just about anything one could grow: raspberry and blueberry bushes, strawberry plants, cantaloupes, corn (which was always knee-high by the 4th of July), asparagus, potatoes, tomatoes, lettuce, beans, peppers, cucumbers and much more, even rhubarb. Garden produce was shared with friends and neighbors. We kids were allowed sometimes to sell eggs, strawberries, or tomatoes to the neighbors. And to keep the profits. Over the years as he gardened, Dad found and collected numerous arrowheads that would have been used by the Mohawk Indians in a prior century. After his death, the collection was donated by the family to the New York State History Museum in Albany.

Five and Done

Three and a half years after moving to 2 Benedict Street, into this very busy but orderly routine, child number five, **Margaret (Peggy) Ann Crist**, was born on January 23, 1941. Some of my brothers enjoyed telling the story of how they were reading comic books when I was brought home from the hospital in a 1939 Ford coupe (Dad's State car) and paid me no attention whatever when I was brought into the house. Probably quite true! In any case, Mom now had her girl which made her happy, but there were to be no more children. The little house was more than full. Five was enough! Moreover, the world was becoming a very scary place, with Hitler on the move in Europe and Japan threatening. Eleven months after I was born, on December 7, the Japanese attacked Pearl Harbor. Jack and Bob were at home and were there when Aunt Ann called to tell Mom about the attack on Pearl Harbor. Jack recalls Mom telling her sister, "*I never did trust the 'Japs'.*" Don also remembers that Sunday. "*For some reason, Dad had taken Dick and I somewhere in the car, and as we came back into the driveway, Mom came running out, waving her hands wildly in the air, saying: (pardon the language), 'Those dirty 'Japs' bombed Pearl Harbor.' We didn't know what it was, but we knew it wasn't good.*" On December 8 the United States declared war on Japan. Three days later Germany and Italy declared war on the United States.

The Way We Were

Growing Up in the 1930s, '40s and '50s

With the war on everyone's mind and many men leaving their families to go "over there" (i.e. the European continent or the Pacific arena), life was instantly more uncertain. For the Crist family life was busier than ever. Bobby and Jackie had started classes at Castleton Union School, where they made the half-mile walk in twelve to fifteen minutes each way twice a day. Children when possible were sent home for lunch. Keep in mind that most moms in those days did not leave the home to go to a job. The school did not have a cafeteria. Paper bag lunches were permitted to be eaten at your desk.

Each weekday morning Mom served a hearty breakfast at the maple table in the dining room. Mom and Dad woke at seven (much earlier for Dad in the winter). Mom dressed in her cotton housedress, apron and shoes (a woman wearing "pants" was very rare in the '40s) and began preparing Dad's breakfast. Dad, in the meantime, had taken those wooden steps into the basement where he stoked the coal furnace by shaking down the burnt coals and adding shovels of fresh coal to warm the house. He would have carefully banked the fire the previous evening to keep it going through the night. For most of our growing up years, coils within the furnace provided our only (limited) supply of hot water. If the fire went out, too bad—no hot water. In the summer months, Dad used a kerosene fire to keep the water hot.

Around seven-fifteen, having dressed, shaved and cleaned up, with the furnace warming the house, Dad sat down to his "Mrs. Harper orange"—named after the owner of tourist cabins where the family had stayed in central New York when Bob and Jack were quite young.

Mrs. Harper prepared breakfast oranges for her guests in one-eighth sections. This forever more became the only acceptable way for the Crist family to eat oranges. As Dad ate his orange, Mom prepared his standing week-day breakfast order: one egg over easy (cooked in the cast iron fry pan in bacon grease), two slices of bacon (not too crisp), and a cup of black coffee—filled to the brim, please. Coffee was prepared by bringing water to a boil in a kettle and then pouring it over the grounds in a drip coffee pot. The hot water then slowly dripped through the grounds to the metal container below which was kept warm on a stovetop burner. Dad was responsible for manning the drop-door toaster on the table and toasting his one slice of Freihofer's white bread (wheat bread hadn't yet gained popularity).

When the shivering children arose around seven-thirty a.m., they usually made a quick stop at The Register on their way to the table. A Mrs. Harper orange, bacon, and maybe an egg awaited. They too toasted their own bread at the table. Butter was a rare treat during the war years of 1941 - 1945. After the war ended, hand-blended margarine was a new and exciting topping for toast. Margarine was packaged in two separate cello squeeze bags, which needed to be blended together to add color to the otherwise unappetizing product. Mom's homemade strawberry, grape, or raspberry jelly was always found on the table.

Somewhere during the morning rush, Mom found time to have her own orange, bacon, egg, toast and cup of coffee and pack four or five lunches for the kids if the weather was especially bad. Dad left the house at eight a.m. after stoking the coal furnace once again and adding enough coal to last the day during the winter months. He drove north from the village on Route 9J, tracking alongside the Hudson on his way to Albany. Each year in the marshes between the river and the road, Pops watched for the red wing blackbirds to return by his birthday on March 6. The red wings rarely disappointed.

The drive continued to 19 Dove Street where his office was located (and where in 2019 there is still an active office of the Health Department) and where his workday began at eight-thirty.

The older children left the house around 8:30 to walk a half mile in all kinds of weather to Castleton Union School at the corner of Scott and Campbell Avenues where school started at eight-fifty a.m. On especially cold mornings, a scarf across your face helped to prevent a frozen nose when you stepped outside, and I remember wearing snow pants on my otherwise bare legs. Girls always wore dresses to school in the '40s.

In warmer months, if you were lucky before leaving for school, Mom offered up a nickel to buy a Fudgesicle at Amsler's store, just a block from school. On a very lucky day there might be a dime to buy a chocolate-covered frost stick.

The two-story brick school building, which is still in use in 2019 for elementary students, housed classrooms for grades one to twelve. Kindergarten was not offered. Elementary grades were located on the first floor. The gymnasium also served as an auditorium with limited balcony seating. A stage area could be created by blocking off the first-floor hallway with sliding curtains and adding risers as needed for school plays, graduation, chorus or band performances. The local Kiwanis Club produced a fundraiser show called The Minstrel each year at the school and which featured local men made up in blackface. To my knowledge, no African Americans lived in Castleton until many years later, nor were any African Americans bused to the school. There was a total of two school buses that brought students from nearby Brookview or Schodack Landing. Everyone else either rode their bike or walked to school.

Many of the teachers served the community for their entire careers and many of the women teachers never married. Spinsters Marian Everleth (first grade), Gertrude Shill (third grade), Corabel Elliott (fourth grade), and Avedia Reid (fifth grade), among others, taught countless numbers of Castleton's elementary grade children over the years. The feared Mrs. Hartman taught sixth grade. Miss Ruth Steele (Latin and math), Mrs. Vivian Ingalls (typing and business), Gerrit Bol (history and social studies), Miss Margaret Ward (English) and George Koerner (science) were long-standing high school teachers at Castleton Union School. Bob Hayes kept everyone in tune during his many years as band and music director. The whole village knew it was in for a treat when the band performed its signature piece: John Phillips Souza's "When the Saints Come Marching In". (No doubt it was my contribution on alto sax that added the magic). Charlie Collins was the legendary coach of the basketball and baseball teams. There were no football, track, volleyball, soccer or swim teams. No one dared to test the patience of Principal Larry Davis, a fit and trim Navy retiree who reportedly had been a boxer in the Navy and was known to use physical enforcement of the rules when necessary. Larry Davis served the school for many years.

A peculiar school-day ritual from the late 1940s and early '50s was the "duck and cover" exercise that we routinely practiced during the school year. Much like a fire drill, during a duck and cover drill, a bell sounded, and the students were instructed to immediately drop to the floor and take cover under our desk. (Desks then were a small table with a separate chair). "Duck and cover" was intended to protect us in the event of a nuclear explosion. That practice has since come under ridicule; as though hiding under a desk would protect anyone from a nuclear explosion. But we all followed the instructions and did as we were told.

***

With Dad and the older children off for their day's efforts, Mom was left to clean the debris of breakfasts and look after the children who hadn't yet started school.

After the children were out the door and the cats and dog had been fed, Mom tackled the day's first load of dirty dishes. She stood at the kitchen sink and washed each dish that had been used that morning: glasses, cups, saucers, plates, knives, forks, spoons, fry pan and coffee pot. Dishes were set to drain on the adjacent drain board and were then dried and put away in the overhead cupboard for the next meal.

Many other chores waited to be tackled. Monday was wash day. The sheets were pulled from each of the six beds first thing in the morning. The Easy Agitator washer was the latest modern convenience and was stored in the spare room adjacent to the kitchen. From the spare room, the washer was rolled through the doorway into the kitchen where it was placed beside the sink. A hose connected to the kitchen sink faucet filled the wash tub with hot water while a second hose allowed the dirty water to drain back into the sink. The hose occasionally became detached and spewed hot water in every direction causing great consternation!

The wash load was placed in the large tub to which soap such as Rinso Blue had been added. Detergents had not yet been invented and washing a load of laundry in cold water was unthinkable. The agitator on the machine swished the laundry until it was determined to be clean. White sheets were always the first load of the day—and sheets were always white.

After the wash and drain cycle was complete, the tub was refilled with rinse water. Following the rinse cycle, each soaking wet item was pulled by hand from the water and hand-fed through a manually operated ringer to squeeze out as much water as possible and with great care not to crush buttons, zippers or fingers. Later machines had a spinner tub which eliminated the need for the wringer. When the process was complete, Mom carried each piece of wet laundry to the window in the spare room. The laundry was hung by leaning out the window, and with the help of a pulley, pushing the clothesline ever further away to where the line was anchored at a height of thirty feet or so on the telephone pole at the far end of the yard. The wet laundry was hung piece by piece with wooden snap clothespins. Several loads of laundry were done each Monday and took many hours of manual labor to accomplish.

After the satisfaction of the laundry being washed and hung, there was always the worry that all that effort might have been in vain. Imagine the horror when Mom would look out at her clean laundry to see it covered with black soot. The locomotives that passed the village burned coal. Occasionally the prevailing wind carried the soot from the trains up the hill to her wash. At which point it was necessary to bring the laundry she had so laboriously washed and hung back inside and start the lengthy process all over again. There weren't too many times over the years that we saw our mother cry, but soot on her clean laundry certainly may have brought on some tears of frustration.

The weather was also a huge factor. Hanging the laundry on a glorious spring or summer day was fine, but not so much on a frigid winter morn when the sheets froze moments after they were hung. Nonetheless, there was no other choice. Electric clothes dryers would not be available for many years. An auxiliary clothesline was available on the side screen porch for back-up use. In the winter months, the clothes were brought back into the house still nearly frozen—usually in the mid-afternoon. Each item was placed, as well as one could, on a collapsible wooden laundry rack which was in turn placed over the register, which was in turn the outlet for the heat from the coal furnace below. The heat output was luscious, and the laundry rack was often crowded out by two or three of the children, along with Tiger and Jigger, the family cats (or Willy and Wiggy as they were also known), and maybe our dog, Chummy. It was the most popular place in the house all winter long.

On Monday, Wednesday, and Friday, Mom's morning

routine was interrupted by the Borden's milkman delivering a metal carrier containing our standing order of eight quarts of fresh pasteurized milk into the back hall. The glass bottles made an unmistakable and charming sound as they clinked together in the carrier. The milk was not homogenized as it is today, which meant that the cream sat on the top of the milk. On a very cold day, the milk would freeze, rise up a couple of inches, and pop the paper top off the milk bottle. In summer, Mom also needed to be alert to when the milk was delivered so it could be put in the refrigerator as soon as possible. Also scheduled to arrive on Monday and Thursday was the Freihofer man, who brought a delectable selection of breads, rolls, cookies, and cakes displayed on a two-tier tray for Mom to choose from. A box of their delicious chocolate chip cookies was a mandatory purchase along with a couple of loaves of bread. Their Louisiana Ring cakes were a great treat for dessert. Some Freihofer and Borden delivery wagons were still horse-drawn in the City of Albany in the 1940s.

The back hall was a small, unheated entry area off the kitchen door. It was a great place to leave wet boots, store anything that didn't need to be in the house, or act as a receiving area for the milk man and the Freihofer man among others. A screen door protected the house from flies and other bugs during the summer and made a loud bang each time it closed. In the winter, Dad replaced the screen door with a storm door. On a rare summer day, a hobo would occasionally knock on the screen door and ask if the lady of the house had any food to spare. Interestingly, as it would be today, this was not a frightening occurrence in the '40s. I recall Mom offered what she could.

A small wood-framed lean-to grape arbor abutted the outside of the back hall and adjoined the roof. Dad had planted grape vines which over the years covered the lean-to and provided great tasting red grapes each fall.

While Mom went about her morning chores, Don

McNeill's "Breakfast Club" filled the nine o'clock hour on the radio. ♫ *Good Morning Breakfast Clubbers, and Howdy-Do Ya'*. A standard gag on the show was Don McNeill heading into the studio audience where he examined and described the contents of ladies' purses to his listeners, while everyone out there in radio-land found the joke to be hilarious. McNeill is credited with being the first performer to bring a talk format to morning radio.

Arthur Godfrey held court on the radio from 10 a.m. to 11:30 a.m. with "Arthur Godfrey and Friends." Julius La Rosa, The McGuire Sisters, Hali Loke, The Chordettes, and Pat Boone were regular performers along with Godfrey's homey chatter and ukulele strumming. Products such as Rinso Blue, Chesterfield cigarettes (buy 'em by the carton!) and Lipton Tea (everybody knows it's the best tea) were advertised. And if Arthur Godfrey liked the product, so did most of the millions of American housewives who wouldn't miss his daily show.

Shortly past noon, the children were back for lunch, having made that half-mile walk home from school. Peanut butter and jelly or baloney sandwiches on white or rye bread, and one or two Freihofer's chocolate chip cookies, along with a glass of Borden's milk, made a fine lunch. Sometimes on a cold day, Mom warmed a can of Campbell's tomato or chicken noodle soup and offered grilled cheese sandwiches made with Velveeta. And on a good day, a new product, Spam, could be fried for sandwiches on white bread with butter. A huge treat. (No one knew about the dangers of saturated fat back then.)

With children back at school and the lunch dishes washed, it was time to think about what to prepare for dinner. It would also soon be time for Mom to open the spare room window, lean out and reel in the clothesline with its loads of laundry needing to be warmed, folded and put away. Art Linkletter's "House Party" which aired beginning in 1944 on CBS Radio, helped lighten the load. His talent with interviewing children led to a successful TV show in later years, "Kids Say the Darndest Things."

The children returned from school around three-fifteen and were soon gone again—often back to school to play. Or down to the ice pond to skate. Or maybe just ride bikes. There was no TV, cell phone or computer to amuse us. At around five-thirty, the sound of crunched gravel in the driveway announced Dad's return from his office, wearing his three-piece suit, white shirt, tie, and brown fedora hat. He would immediately head to his bedroom and change into work clothes and shoes. In the winter, the coal furnace needed prompt attention.

If it was summer, corn was likely ripe in the garden and ready to pick. Dad headed to the garden, did some hoeing and weeding and at the appointed hour (about ten before six), enough fresh picked and husked corn for all the family (several ears each for the boys) was delivered to the kitchen where a large pot of boiling water awaited. The boys were also very good at husking the corn. The corn was cooked for eight minutes—no more, no less. If strawberries were ripe, the children were expected to pick at least six quarts of fresh berries for dessert that night. It was Mom's job to wash and hull the berries and sprinkle them with confectionary sugar, although help was usually available from one or more of the kids.

Dinner was always on the table at six. Dad sat at the far end with his back to the screen porch, Mom at the opposite end nearest the kitchen. Bob sat beside Dad facing the spare room with Jack beside him. The twins sat opposite Bob and Jack facing the living room, with Don closer to Dad. My place was beside Mom at the narrow end of the table (in the early years in my highchair.) And if Dad told the boys once, he told them a hundred times, "Do not tip back on your chairs." But some of them did anyway. Discussions at the table included everything from the day's activities to school to sports to politics. Mom had strong political views. Dick created a nickname that stuck—"Senator Margaret Chase Mim" (a take-off on the U.S. Senator from Maine, Margaret Chase Smith. Senator Smith was an outspoken supporter of women's rights and a strong opponent of McCarthyism in the '50s.) Jack remembers that Mom had issues with FDR (although she may have voted for him at least once), and she did not care for Harry Truman, which was not unusual at the time. She definitely voted for the hugely popular Republican Dwight Eisenhower. And I would imagine that she strongly supported the Irish Catholic Democrat, John Fitzgerald Kennedy. I think Dad remained a staunch Republican throughout the years.

There was ALWAYS a family meal each day—no exceptions. Monday through Thursday, the dinner meal consisted of meat such as pork chops, lamb chops, chuck steaks or the occasional chicken fried in Crisco in the cast iron skillet. Boiled potatoes were most always part of the meal. Fresh vegetables from the garden in the summer or perhaps some of Mom's canned green beans or a can of corn or peas in the winter added to the meal. Plenty of good fresh food for all to enjoy. Sunday dinner would typically be a fine roast of beef or a roasted chicken with mashed potatoes and vegetable. And a glass or two of milk was always part of the kids' meal. Never soda!

Bread was rarely found on the Crist dinner table. Dad often said, "Bread at dinner is for the poor people." Other items that never appeared on the 2 Benedict Street table were spaghetti (I ate my first spaghetti dinner at a restaurant on a date when I was about twenty-two years old), or rice. I never remember Mom cooking either spaghetti or rice in all the years at home. This was, after all, a German/Irish home where potatoes ruled. Lastly, I do not remember ever having soda on hand for the kids or adults. Jack remembers Dad calling soda pop (as it was known at the time) "poison pop."

Catholic canon law did not permit the faithful to eat meat on Fridays, so Friday was when everyone looked forward to a huge dish of Mom's own recipe—eggs and noodles. This treat was always served with tuna fish salad and hot stewed tomatoes. (Eggs and noodles are still enjoyed in many Crist homes.) No one had ever heard of pizza, Thai or Mexican food. Carry-out would be invented in another twenty years or so!

A cup of hot tea in the winter (or a glass of homemade iced tea in the summer) and a dessert such as canned peaches or pears (and possibly one or two Freihofer's chocolate chip cookies) completed the meal when strawberries were not in season. After dinner, Mom faced the third set of dirty dishes of the day, and after washing and drying them, put them away to be ready for the morning's breakfast. Although we kids did not have many assigned chores, it was pretty typical that one of us would help with drying the dishes after dinner, if we weren't off to an evening school event or other activity.

After dinner, homework was overseen, fights were refereed, card houses were built and "accidentally" destroyed, and games of War or Go Fish were played—all on that durable dining room table. Monopoly, checkers, poker and the new card game, Canasta, were often played on Saturday night as we breathlessly awaited news of the number one hit of the week on "Your Lucky Strike Hit Parade," a sixty-minute radio show heard on NCB each Saturday. Snooky Lanson, Russell Arms, Dorothy Collins, and Gisele MacKensey presented their renditions of the top ten songs of the past week in a countdown format and ended the show each week with the trademark song, ♫ *"So long for a while, that's all the songs for a while, so long from your Hit Parade and the songs that you picked to be played. So long."*

Don often disappeared in the evenings only to be found at the small table in the closet in his bedroom. There he spent hours creating model airplanes from balsa wood and glue. Definitely a preview of what would come in later life. In his teen years, Dick loved to spend hours and hours shooting hoops at the outdoor court at school. Bob, at ten years my senior, was busy with his high school friends and school activities. Don would often thumb a ride to the nearby airport after school and on weekends where he worked in trade for flying lessons.

Bob and Jack spent countless hours together tinkering with old cars and prepping them for nearby Saturday night stock car races.

Although my big brothers kept busy with their own interests and hobbies, all the boys were there to defend me if anyone outside the family tried to pick on their little sister. I always knew my brothers had my back if I needed them, even if Dick did enjoy teasing me when he could.

Because I was the youngest, I was given great freedom (by my busy mom) to make my own plans with my neighborhood friends and later with my school friends. I was never told I couldn't go "play with" anyone or that I needed to stay home to clean my room, do my homework, or any other activity. I believe this freedom is the source of the independence I have felt throughout my life and possibly the reason I had no fear of setting off to live in Europe at age twenty-three. Rarely do I recall being disciplined. But I do clearly remember being spanked once. Somewhere around five or six years old, I was upset about something. I decided I would "show them" and announced I was going to run away. I ran out the kitchen door, through the back hall, and into the driveway as I was thinking, OK, now what do I do? The answer was to run around to the front porch and reenter the house through the living room door. My mother sat down on a dining room chair and put me over her lap to administer the discipline. I don't recall ever wanting to run away again.

***

While washing and drying the evening dishes, Mom listened to "One Man's Family," "Just Plain Bill," "Young Widow Brown," "The Guiding Light," "The Romance of Helen Trent," "Stella Dallas" and many other soap operas which aired in fifteen-minute segments beginning at seven p.m. The kitchen radio sat atop the Frigidaire refrigerator.

On laundry day, once the sheets had warmed enough

over the register to be placed back on the beds, usually after dinner, Mom remade each bed with the crisp, fresh-smelling and toasty sheets before tucking us in with a kiss on the forehead. A very long and tiring day—repeated each Monday. The words "I love you" were not part of the daily dialog as they are in the twenty-first century, but each of us knew as a certainty that we were loved by both of our parents. Their love was demonstrated when they showed up for their "jobs" seven days a week no matter what and did their absolute best to provide a good life for their children. And we children, for the most part, would not think of committing an act that would bring shame to the family.

Baths or showers were not yet a daily occurrence for many families in this era—especially families with five kids and one bathroom with no shower and only limited hot water.

The large wooden console RCA radio (first in the dining room and later in the living room) aired shows such as "The Shadow," "The Green Hornet," "The Lone Ranger," "Jack Armstrong - The All American Boy" and "Captain Midnight," after dinner beginning at seven p.m. The children gathered around the radio and absorbed every sound that The Shadow made. Radio programming required the listeners to use their own imaginations to envision the characters in the story they were hearing.

"The Great Gildersleeve," "Amos and Andy," "Fibber McGee and Molly, "Our Miss Brooks" and so many more were all popular evening entertainment in the eight o'clock hour. Dad loved The Jack Benny show which was followed by Fred Allen on Sunday nights. Interestingly, radios then had the ability to tune in far distant high frequency stations—even as far as England.

TV didn't arrive at 2 Benedict Street until the very late 1940s or early '50s. Occasionally before we had our own TV, Uncle John Crist would invite us to his home on Croswell Street in Albany to view the "Cavalcade of Sports Friday Night Fights." This was a hugely popular show and

Pops loved to watch while visiting John and Kathryn. A small magnifier was set up in front of the even smaller TV screen for better viewing. Gillette sponsored these shows each week and their theme song, ♬ *"To Look Sharp and be on the Ball, To Feel Sharp When You Hear the Call, Just Be Sharp! Use Gillette Blue Blades for the cleanest, neatest shave of all"* was well known to every one of the era.

During the war years, we learned what must be done in the event an air raid drill was sounded. The town fire sirens would sound a long and continuous blast. This meant that everything needed to be darkened immediately. All house lights were to be turned off and shades pulled for additional darkening. The drill would last only a relatively short time, maybe fifteen minutes or so. These drills became a matter of routine and everyone complied as needed. Dad served for a time as an air raid warden whose duty was to check for any stray light showing from nearby homes.

Dad grew corn for popping in his garden as a special treat for the family. The ears of ripe corn were stored in the basement during the winter. Whenever I had a craving to eat popcorn, I simply went down the stairs into the basement and chose an ear of popcorn. After removing the individual kernels from the husk, they were put into a metal pot along with a healthy dab of Crisco. Before long a very full bowl of fresh and delicious popcorn was ready, needing only butter and salt to make it perfect, a habit that was repeated almost nightly over the years I grew up.

At nine or nine-thirty, the children were off to their bedrooms; the twins in their twin beds in the back-upstairs bedroom, Bob and Jack in the downstairs bedroom in twin beds, while I was assigned the spare room. (As a baby, my crib was in the closet of Dick and Don's room. And if memory serves me correctly, I stayed in the crib until I started school).

After dinner was over, Dad read the Albany

Knickerbocker News followed by a nap in his chair. Mom and I were on the couch with Mom possibly reading me a story (*Fraidy Cat* was a favorite) or looking through the latest *Saturday Evening Post* with a marvelous cover by Norman Rockwell, or *Life Magazine*, filled with prize-winning photos from all over the world. And by then the evening was pretty much over for everyone. Dad's last duty was to place one or two shovels of coal into the furnace around eleven p.m. I often needed reassurance at bedtime that Dad would remember to turn the flame down on the kerosene water heater. Once or twice it had flared up and nearly caught the old wooden ceiling timbers on fire.

Dad's hearing was poor for much of his adult life and he wore a hearing aid to compensate. His hearing aid was about the size of a pack of cigarettes and was kept in his shirt pocket. After a long day, Dad enjoyed removing the earpiece from his ear and letting it dangle on his shirt. If Dad neglected to turn off the hearing aid, a loud screech emanated from the unused earpiece as he dozed. Sometimes an "accidental" bump into his leg would alert him to turn off the hearing aid.

Such was the daily routine at 2 Benedict Street. Mom's Tuesday chores included more laundry if it hadn't all been finished on Monday due to bad weather or other interferences. Unending piles of shirts and slacks which had been sprinkled with water, wrapped in a towel and kept in the refrigerator until there was time to iron, and housecleaning chores always awaited, along with the general running of the household.

Mom wasn't inclined to be a "joiner." I remember her telling me that she would get calls to join the local ladies' groups in Castleton (The Eastern Star comes to mind) which she never accepted. The one exception to this rule was her bi-weekly bridge club of which she was a member for over thirty years. Mom was interested primarily in taking care of her family and enjoying her home without a lot of outside commitments. Her closeness with her sister Ann was very important to her and a much-needed daily chat was mandatory (HE 9-1793) to share the joys and frustrations of life.

Mom's personality was such that, although she may have felt beaten down and overburdened on occasion, her strong Irish roots gave her the strength to carry on with her duties even when life was tough. She typically did not openly vent her feelings about challenges and difficult times, but there certainly were exceptions. Nothing angered her more than someone mistreating one of her children. If there was an issue at school with one of us, Mom would drop her daily chores, change from her housedress into a nicer dress along with her girdle and stockings, put her lipstick and earrings on ("I don't feel dressed without my earrings.") and walk up to the school to confront Principal Larry Davis about whatever injustice had occurred. Mom was also a big worrier. If there was any chance one of her brood was in danger, the worry would consume her until the perceived danger had passed.

***

When Marge and Rob moved to Castleton, their friends and family all still lived in Albany and Dad worked in Albany. At the time, a phone call to Albany from a Castleton line was billed as a long-distance call. Mom knew that she would be making and receiving many phone calls to and from Albany. For that reason, they arranged to have an Albany phone number (5-4076) that would allow these calls to be billed as local calls and not long-distance, which would have gotten expensive. The only way to accomplish having an Albany line was to understand and agree that it would be a "party" line. A party line, in this case, meant six other customers were sharing the same phone line. As it turned out, one of the other users of our party line was the local hardware store with Garry Roozeboom as the proprietor. When businessman Garry would pick up the phone and heard

Marge talking with Ann, for instance, he would loudly curse that "the damn women are on the phone again" and slam the receiver loudly back on the phone. Oh, and any call could be listened to by any other user of the party line at any time.

***

An infamous moment in history occurred on Sunday, October 30, 1938. Orson Welles broadcast a radio adaptation of H.G. Wells' classic *War of the Worlds* without a disclaimer that it was merely a work of fiction. The unusual staging of the production added to the authenticity of the show. Orson Welles and his producers had listened again and again to the recording of the Hindenburg disaster and patterned their broadcast after that show. The broadcast, which aired in bulletin format, used the studio's emergency fill-in music during airtime gaps to add to the reality of the broadcast.

Nationwide hysteria ensued as the very dramatic descriptions of the object that landed in New Jersey aired:

"An artificial cylinder that opens, disgorging Martians who are big and greyish with oily brown skin, the size, perhaps, of a bear, each with two large dark-colored eyes, and lipless V-shaped mouths which drip saliva and are surrounded by two Gorgon groups of tentacles."

The story line was that the aliens had "terrifying war machines," which had landed in Mountain Lakes, New Jersey and were heading up the Hudson River and killing everyone along the way. The drama aired at eight p.m. and continued for sixty minutes.

At 2 Benedict Street, Mom received a phone call from her sister, Ann, in Delmar. Mom was sobbing as she answered and told Ann to turn the radio on immediately. Their brother Bill and his family lived in Mountain Lakes at the time and were now assumed to be dead. As this hysteria was unfolding, Mom urged Dad to get the kids into the car while Dad famously grabbed his shotguns and headed to the front porch. He will evermore be remembered as bravely saying, "I'm going to get some of them before they get me." As the conversation with Ann progressed, however, Ann said her family was listening to the comedy of Edgar Bergan and Charlie McCarthy on another station. Slowly it dawned that this was all a hoax.

It goes without saying that Orson Welles was not a popular person for many years to come.

Provisioning Day

Mom and Dad's household financial system operated on a cash basis. Dad received a paper check every two weeks which he cashed at his bank (electronic transfers to checking accounts were not available). Dad gave Mom a fixed amount of cash which was to last for the coming two weeks. This was Mom's total "allowance" with which she ran the household and, by today's standards, was extremely minimal. It covered groceries, the Freihofer man and Borden milk man, doctor and dentist visits, school fees, clothing and shoes for the family, piano lessons, sports equipment, linens and household items, Charge-a-card bills, and multiple other expenses. There was no alternate fund source. Mom's allowance was all that was available to her. If there were extraordinary expenses in a given month, bills would take longer to be paid—though they always were paid.

Credit cards were not yet in popular use and Dad was always proud to say he never owned one. The large department stores on Pearl Street in Albany each participated in a system called "Charge-a-card." This card was accepted as payment in a half-dozen or so Albany stores which then billed the owner monthly.

Dad's portion of his check covered taxes, car purchases, repairs and gas, insurance, coal for heating the house, house repairs, his lunches, vacations, and of course, Olga's chili on a Saturday night—among all the other expected and unexpected costs of living. I never once thought of us as being poor, but there sure wasn't a lot of extra cash for luxuries. And I never, ever recall hearing a discussion between Mom and Dad about finances—good or bad. They had their system and it worked.

Friday was shopping day. Because this was a one-car family (as were most families of the era), Dad needed the car for the daily drive to his office in Albany. Mom also needed the car at least once a week to travel to the grocery stores in Albany and do other errands. The grocery stores in Castleton were considered to be more expensive than the larger stores in Albany and not as well stocked.

The Friday routine was always the same. After the children left for school, Mom washed the dishes, got herself and any loose children still at home dressed and began the eight to ten-minute walk to the bus stop at Seaman and Campbell Avenues. Benedict Street was still unpaved at the time and there were only a few scattered houses. Large potholes made watchfulness necessary while walking, and the street was often not well plowed in the winter. A right on Boltwood followed by a left on Seaman, past the large house and office of Dr. Spieski (the feared town dentist) to Campbell Avenue where the bus line (a total of two buses) made regular pick-ups at eleven a.m., if they were on time.

The repurposed school bus traveled out Brookview Road to East Greenbush, up the hill past the cemetery on the right where Citizen Genet is buried, and down the State Road across the Dunn Memorial Bridge into Albany. Passengers disembarked at The Plaza in front of the D & H building in downtown Albany. (The building stands today. From William Kennedy: *"This is a majestic structure that is a copy of the Clothmakers Guild Hall in Ypres, Belgium."* It was designed by Albany's greatest twentieth-century architect, Marcus T. Reynolds, in conjunction with the Delaware and Hudson Railroad.) The trip took about a half-hour and may have cost twenty-five or fifty cents per person.

From the Plaza, Mom and the children walked up

State Street hill to the corner of State and Pearl in front of Walgreen's Drug Store and caught a city bus up to Dove Street. After retrieving the car key from Dad (or finding it under the floor mat), the trip continued to the Albany Public Market at 652 Central Avenue. The store later relocated after the war to 711 Central and was hailed at the time as "the largest food department store in the world" and was said to be able to hold several B-29 bombers!

Frozen foods had been invented in 1924 but selections were very limited for many years, so most everything Mom bought was fresh and somehow needed to last a full week. During the war years, it was necessary to carry a War Ration Card when shopping for everything from gas to sugar to shoes. A fine of 10,000 1940 dollars was threatened for those who misused their card. Mom was pleased when the butcher at The Trading Port at 309 Central Avenue gave her a little extra butter or an extra pork chop on the side for her large family. In the smaller markets, products were purchased by lining up at a counter and requesting the items on your list. As Mom shopped for ingredients to prepare meals for the week ahead, she would often remark, "I wish they would invent a new kind of meat." There were only so many times you could eat pork chops or lamb chops without being bored by them.

Around four forty-five it was time to head back to 19 Dove Street where Dad was finishing his day at the office. Stops might also have been made at John G. Myers or W. M. Whitney's, the large department stores on North Pearl Street, where clothing or household goods could be purchased. In the twenties, Whitney's advertised that they were one of the first major department stores in the country to feature electric lights, elevators, and telephones. Thom McAn's shoe store was beside Myers; and Lodge's, also on North Pearl (and still open in 2019), was the perfect place to shop for clothing necessities such as socks and underwear.

John G. Myers had opened his business on Pearl Street in the late 1800s. Following his death in 1901 the store continued to expand into a high-quality department store which remained in business until 1970. It was an iconic place to shop, and I have great memories of my mother taking me to the store. The various departments included clothing for the family, jewelry, furniture, linens, dishes and kitchen supplies, among others. "Notions" was a favorite department and was where one could purchase odds and ends such as thread and sewing supplies, or seasonal decorations. A soda fountain for sandwiches and ice cream was found in the basement. As a special treat when Mom had time, I loved having my favorite lunch there: grilled cheese sandwich, French fries and a delicious hot fudge sundae. Still favorites in my life seventy-five years later.

The elevators were manned by a seated and uniformed operator who would announce "Third Floor – Ladies Lingerie" or whatever as the elevator neared its destination. Throughout the six-story building, a shopper would find well-attired women behind wooden and glass cases displaying everything from fine china and silverware to nylon stockings. A woman desiring to make a selection at the nylons counter would be met by a lady clerk with a perfect manicure. Several boxes of nylons were placed on the counter before the customer. The clerk would then carefully insert her hand, made into a knuckle, several inches into the stocking and spread her fingers to display the color and denier (the measurement of weight and strength) of the hose as the shopper carefully made her selection.

With the end of World War II in the mid-40s, nylon stockings became widely available and mandatory attire for women. A dark seam running the length of the stocking on the back of the leg was very fashionable. If a woman's seam was not straight, it was an offense worthy of taking her aside to whisper that "Your seams are crooked." Immediate repairs were made in the privacy of a rest room. And a run in your nylons could create panic in an otherwise wonderful outing. ("I have a run in my stocking!") Stockings (or hose) were attached to either a girdle or a garter belt around the waist. Pantyhose wouldn't be available for years yet to come.

F. W. Woolworth's Five and Dime was at 69 North Pearl while Kresge's at 15 North Pearl was nearby and was always the place to buy dried fruit for making Mom's annual fruit cake. Snappy Men's Shop on South Pearl Street was the perfect spot to choose a Christmas or birthday gift for one of the boys. There were no cash registers on the sales floor in many stores. Rather, pneumatic tubes were used to transfer the money. The hand-written sales receipt and cash were placed in the tube which then ascended (with a lovely whooshing sound) to a horizontal track under the ceiling and arrived in an unseen office where a clerk made change and sent the receipt and any change back to the sales clerk to pass along to the customer. The system worked quite well.

The shops closed at five p.m. Monday thru Saturday, with the exception of Thursday, when the stores stayed open until nine p.m. Everything was closed on Sunday.

If the weather was nice and there were a few extra minutes that could be squeezed into the day before picking up Dad, Mom would make a stop at Washington Park to allow the kids to play on the iconic four-person "gondola" wooden swings or to feed the ducks in the lake.

After returning home, groceries were unloaded, kids were set free to play and it was time to start dinner (see eggs and noodles above.) And then clean up from dinner. Another very long day for Mom. In all kinds of weather. And whether she felt well or not. And whether the kids were sick or not. Had to be done.

Pizza wasn't available in Castleton until the early to mid '50s. Going out to dinner was unheard of for the family. McDonalds and other fast food chains had yet to be invented and families with many children couldn't usually afford to eat in nicer restaurants. Many years later, Dad and I would make a Friday afternoon stop after work at Walter Foods on Washington Avenue just north of my office at 881 Madison Avenue for several take-out servings of their famous fried haddock. It was as fresh as could be and delicious—a wonderful treat for no-meat Fridays and gave Mom a night away from the stove.

Weekends were very different. Everything was much more laid back. Saturdays were always cereal days—no hot kitchen on Saturday morning.

Men like John Kellogg and C. W. Post had developed a new product known as cereal in the late 1800s and early 1900s. Cold cereal emerged on the market during the '20s and quickly became popular with American families. Puffed Rice, Puffed Wheat, Cheerios, Corn Flakes, Rice Krispies or Wheaties "The Breakfast of Champions," were often on the Crist family table to choose from. The first to open a new box of cereal dug his or her hand to the bottom in search of the "prize" which could be anything from a whistle to a small toy.

Don remembers Saturday afternoons:

"When we ran out of 'strawberry money', Mom would find an extra dime that she would give each of us (usually just Dick & I) so we could go to the Saturday matinee movies on the second floor of the I.O.O.F Building on Main Street. For ten cents, the afternoon always began with the latest update from Movietone News "World News Today" which was the only option for people who wanted to see film of current events and was frequently narrated by the distinctive baritone of Lowell Thomas. A cartoon comedy or two were next, followed by the previews for next week and finally the feature film began—often a Western starring Hopalong Cassidy or Roy Rogers. Plus, if memory serves me, the dime also got you a candy bar!"

***

Dinner, too, was a much less formal event on Saturday. Often, hamburgers, hot dogs and home-made French fries were on the menu. It was one such night when Mom was making French fries in her cast iron skillet on the electric stove that she sustained a terrible burn. The Crisco in the pan was about three inches deep—enough to completely cover the potatoes with the boiling fat. Mom's attention was diverted long enough that the grease overheated and caught fire. The pan was at a full blaze when she picked it up, carried it out the kitchen through the back hall and slung the flaming grease away from her into the yard. Tragically, the arcing motion of the pan caused the burning grease to fly backward and cause a very serious burn on the entire length of Mom's right arm below the elbow. Dad drove her to Dr. Sydney Kimmelblot's home office on South Main Street to be treated. The enormous blister ran from her inner wrist to her elbow. It was a very painful experience and took some time to completely heal.

(Dr. Kimmelblot was known to be short with people and did not seem to have great empathy for the afflicted. But he was our doctor. The second doctor in town, Dr. Austen, was the school doctor and wasn't as highly regarded by our family. "Kimmie," as he was known locally, was a pioneer in the use of penicillin in the mid-40s and was credited for administering the first dose of penicillin used in Albany to a critically ill woman. The drug was brand new and in scarce supply as most all available quantities went to the troops to sustain the war effort.)

***

At one point in the early '50s, the family made an exciting new purchase: a record player! I remember clearly its white plastic housing and Jack reminds me that the sound was produced by connecting the record player to the RCA console radio that sat nearby. The sound came through the radio speakers. Saturday was a good night to turn on the record player. Twelve-inch 78 rpm vinyl phonograph records were played one at a time. The new 45 rpms came later. Though it is not possible to mention all the wonderful songs we grew up with, anything by Glen Miller; "In the Mood," and "Pennsylvania Six Five 000" come to mind along with Artie Shaw and pop songs such as "So Rare" or "I'm Looking Over a Four-Leaf Clover." Vaughn Monroe's version of "Dance Ballerina Dance" was haunting and Bing Crosby's new recording of "White Christmas" was must-listening. Mom loved anything sung by an Irish tenor. I could fill ten pages with the songs we loved.

Dad would often head to McGivern's American House, Clinton's, or Len Deering's Village Inn on a Saturday night. At Clintons he could order a bowl of Olga's chili. "Hot enough to bring a drop of sweat to the brow," according to Dad. A few beers along with the chili, a game or two of darts, and he came home a happy man. Mom was just happy that she didn't have the usual big weeknight meal to prepare.

***

Dad had long dreamed of owning a small farm with animals such as chickens or goats, and planting an acre or two of vegetables. At one point when I was maybe in third or fourth grade, Dad found a farm that was for sale in nearby Muitzeskill. Jack recalls that the property sat at the end of a long dirt driveway. Dad very much wanted to sell 2 Benedict Street and move to this farm. Mom had the wisdom to know that this would be a catastrophic move for the children who had the village of friends, school and activities at their fingertips, and for herself. The idea of becoming a farmer's wife with five children in a remote area with one car was completely unpalatable to Mom. And though I don't recall hearing them discuss this possibility, I do know with certainty that Mom uncharacteristically put her foot down and said it was not happening. Thank you, Mom!

Let us Pray

The first Saturday of each month meant it was time for Marge and the children to drive one and a half miles up Benedict Street, past the school on Campbell Avenue, past the Lutheran Church on Green Avenue and over to Sacred Heart Church at the top of Stimpson Avenue for seven p.m. confession with Father Francis J. Gustompski, known as Father Gus. Sacred Heart had been built in 1887 and sits majestically on a hill overlooking the Hudson River. A circular drive surrounds the church and a parish house sits beside the ancient cemetery. The church's red brick and granite block exterior with a black slate roof is complemented by a huge steeple on the front left side of the building. Two wide stairways lead to matching double-wide heavy wooden arched doors which allow entry into the church vestibule. The interior contains eighteen hand-hewn oak pews on each side, seating approximately 250 people. Large arched stained-glass windows line both sides of the church while a hand-painted mural lined both side walls above the windows and the apse. Small altars on each side of the main altar feature life-size statues of Mary and Joseph. The apse contains two large arched windows on either side and a glorious mural of Jesus surrounded by Angels appears behind the main altar. At the opposite end of the church, a large stained-glass window fills the rear wall in the choir loft. Perhaps the most impressive aspect of the interior design is the imposing tongue in groove dark walnut ceiling with open heavy walnut truss supports and balusters throughout. Hand-carved finials add to the stunning appearance of the ceiling. Five walnut support arms attach to the walls at midpoint on both sides of the church between the stained-glass windows. Four original black metal pendant lanterns on both sides of the church provide the lighting.

Penitents were expected to enter the dimly lit, mostly empty church through the side door, and take a pew on the right side near the confessional and behind those who had previously arrived. Silence was the order of the evening while the congregants contemplated their sins and awaited their turn to go behind the heavy curtain into one of the two small darkened confessional chambers.

There, behind a small screen in the dim light of the sacristy, sat Father Gus dressed in a traditional all-black cassock. Only his head and upper body were visible as he opened the sliding door and waited for the recitation of your sins. "Bless Me Father for I Have Sinned. It has been xxx weeks since my last confession" was always the opening dialog as you knelt before Father. I remember as a young child having no idea what sins were. I once made up a story that I stole a pencil in school just so I would have something to confess to. After the sins were recited, absolution was granted, and your penance, usually five or ten Our Father's and Hail Mary's, was declared, you were free to head to the communion rail, say your prayers and head home feeling quite purified. Those waiting in the pews for their turn with Father Gus sometimes silently observed how long a previously absolved sinner remained at the altar rail. If the time was longer than usual, suspicions were made about the gravity of the penitent's sins.

Mass was said each Sunday at eight and ten a.m. with the eight a.m. service being High Mass on the first Sunday of the month. All masses were said in Latin. High Mass was accompanied by the organist and the choir from the loft above the parishioners. Getting herself and the five children—awake, dressed, and ready—to church for first-Sunday Communion before eight was not an easy task for Mom. Before she left for Mass, Mom prepared breakfast for Dad who stayed behind. He had been raised as a member of the Dutch Reformed Church in Albany and did his praying at home.

The rest of the family was not allowed to eat breakfast until after Communion was taken at Mass. Eating or drinking anything, including water, after midnight on a Communion day was forbidden by the church. This rule was strictly obeyed. It didn't matter if you were hungry or thirsty. I can still remember the guilty feeling I had from occasionally taking a tiny sip of water before Mass.

The family arrived at Sacred Heart in all kinds of weather wearing their Sunday best. Mrs. Crist and her five children could most always be found midpoint on the left side of the church and often in a pew behind where the Carney family sat with their four girls, Marian, Lucille, Betty and Fran. Or, if Mom was running late, the very front pew was often available, necessitating that embarrassing long walk down the side aisle in full view of the entire parish—and the priest who didn't miss a thing. The church was almost always full with familiar faces for both the eight a.m. and ten a.m. services.

Women were required to cover their heads with a hat, or if a hat wasn't available, a pretty hankie could serve the purpose. In the early '60s, Spanish lace mantillas became very fashionable after Jackie Kennedy was photographed wearing one. Some of the women parishioners wore furs in the winter along with their stylish hats and gloves. Spinster sisters Helen and Mary Lynch always brought a touch of glamour to Sacred Heart in the right front pews with their beautiful mink stoles and half-veiled hats while Viola Meany's full skin (including the face) fox wrap always needed studying, especially during the sermon. If the roads were bad with snow, the family walked to church. There were probably fewer than a half-dozen times over the years that the Crist family missed Mass.

The Latin Mass began, "*In Nomine Patris et Filii and Spiritus Sanctum,*" prayers were said, the Gospel was read, the sermon was given, Jack Ray and Arty Scroi passed the collection baskets as the congregation recited the Nicene Creed, lines were formed for communion, Bert and Kitty Murphy and Bill Hartnagel's fine voices joined Eleanor Lavin's and others' in the choir, the second collection was taken, "Go, the Mass has ended" was declared, and by nine a.m. it was time to go home. Upon returning home, Mom immediately prepared breakfast for her hungry brood. Each and every Sunday morning for over thirty years, the menu consisted of one-half of a grapefruit, sections loosened and with sugar sprinkled on top, along with lots of pancakes made on the cast-iron griddle (never blueberry and certainly never **ever** chocolate chip), Aunt Jemima maple syrup generously applied, and First Prize chunky sausage links on each plate. Always a big hit for the hungry family.

On the remaining Sundays of the month, the family attended the ten a.m. Mass and had the luxury of having breakfast (see above) before they left for church. After Mass, Sister Judith and the other nuns taught Sunday School in the choir loft or in the basement classrooms. The nuns wore habits of black serge fabric draped to the floor; a white starched linen wimple covered the neck and upper chest, and a white headpiece wrapped tightly across the forehead while a black serge veil covered the head and fell to the ankles. A woven black wool belt and the nun's large wooden rosary hung from the waist, while a silver cross hung around the neck.

Don remembers: *Dick and I became altar boys for Father Gus sometime late in the war years, maybe when we were about nine. We did it for about three years. We'd serve seven a.m. Mass for six straight days from Monday through Saturday, and then serve the ten a.m. Mass on Sunday. We'd have the next week 'off', until starting all over again with the Sunday eight a.m. Mass. On a typical day, Dick and I walked the one and a half miles from home to the church (either the uptown route or downtown along Main Street and up the hundred or so old iron steps from Stimson Avenue) and then back home for breakfast, before walking the half mile from home to Castleton Union School. Most often we'd also walk the one-mile round-trip home for lunch, and then back to school until three or so. Then it was back home to change clothes, and very often—back to school again to play with 'the gang.' And it wasn't at all unusual for us to go back to school after dinner on a nice evening for more playing—the school had the only outdoor basketball court in town. No carpools—EVER! Just excellent times, with lots of exercise.*

***

Father Lawler replaced Father Gus in 1953. Father Joseph P. Conway assisted in the Parish for many years and eventually was elevated to Monsignor. Sacred Heart Church became a special place of family significance beyond Sunday Mass. First communions, confirmations, and in later years weddings and funerals of family and friends were all an integral part of life. A weekly evening visit to say The Stations of the Cross was expected during Lent, and three p.m. Good Friday services were events not to be missed and necessitated taking the afternoon off from work if possible. Major hotels in Albany ran notices in the newspapers that neither music nor dancing would be offered on Good Friday. The church still stands proudly atop the hill overlooking the village below with the river beyond, perhaps in need of a bit of refreshing, but still beautiful today.

It's Over, Over There

Victory in Europe, V-E Day, was declared by the Allies following the Nazi's unconditional surrender on the 8th of May 1945. As a four-year old at the time, I remember all the neighbors joyously gathering in our front yard and driveway. The rejoicing was repeated in cities, including Albany, throughout the country and throughout the world as people gathered to celebrate the end of the war in Europe. Times Square in New York City erupted with millions of rapturous people.

The war in the Pacific would go on for another three months. President Harry Truman approved the use of the first atomic bomb which was dropped on Hiroshima,

Japan on August 6. Three days later a second atomic bomb was dropped on Nagasaki. Emperor Hirohito of Japan surrendered on August 14th, which became known as V-J Day, Victory in Japan. On September 2, 1945 a formal surrender ceremony was held aboard the *U.S.S. Missouri* in Tokyo Bay, Japan.

The world again rejoiced with the ending of the Pacific War. Of course, I did not understand what was happening or why everyone was so happy, but I do clearly remember joining in the fun by doing somersaults in the driveway. Jack remembers Dad and Mom piling everyone into the car and driving to State and Pearl Streets in Albany near the Ten Eyck Hotel where a huge crush of tens of thousands of people celebrated that the war was over and "the boys" would soon be coming home again. Or as Dad had predicted in his song, "When the War Is Over, I'll Come Back to You." Don remembers the occasion to be the first time Dad allowed him to fire a shot gun and "*It knocked me on my butt.*"

A letter dated August 21, 1945 sent by Isabel Pawluk, a parishioner at St. Casmir's in Albany, to the father of Albanian John Murawski who was serving in Guam, describes the scene in Albany: "*Your home town went wild for a night—bells rang, whistles blew, fireworks exploded, people laughed and cried—all at the same time. Multitudes of people thronged the churches to give thanks. Of course, the grills were busy too!*"

Don remembers walking home from altar boy duty at Sacred Heart one Saturday morning in 1946 or '47: "*We passed the railroad station at the bottom of Scott Avenue and saw a lot of activity near the stopped train. Quickly we realized what it was all about—some uniformed soldiers were taking several flag-draped coffins off the train while the families of the deceased soldiers stood by. The war had ended several years earlier, and these young men were coming home to the States for the last time. Sobering for a twelve-year-old.*"

The Holidays

Easter

Good Catholics and others of faith were expected to fast during the six-week period of Lent which ended on Easter Sunday. Giving up chocolate was a popular sacrifice to make for Lent while some brave folks gave up smoking. The very brave ones swore off alcohol. Easter morning for the Crists began with eight a.m. High Mass at Sacred Heart (following confession the night before). One did not attend Easter Mass without sporting a fine spring outfit accented by a wonderful bonnet for the ladies and girls. For a young girl like me, patent leather shoes and purse were to match, while a hat and white gloves accented the dress. Corsages were very popular in the late '50s and early '60s. I recall on several occasions giving my mom an orchid corsage on Easter morning. Each man wore his finest white shirt, tie and suit. Casual attire was unthinkable.

Back home after Mass, breakfast was prepared by Mom and five Easter baskets magically appeared on the dining room table. Soon preparations for Easter dinner were underway. Roast leg of lamb with mint jelly (along with the ever-popular boiled potatoes) and a vegetable (possibly asparagus from the garden) was a good choice. A large baked ham was another great choice. Uncle Eddie and Aunt Ann, along with Joanne and Grandma Dennin, sometimes joined us for dinner or possibly just dessert after dinner had ended.

The 4th of July

The 4th of July was a low-key holiday in Castleton. If the 4th happened to fall on a weekend day, we would likely have gone swimming at the dam or at Knickerbocker Lake during the day. More than likely hamburgers and hot dogs were cooked on an outside grill and dinner would be picnic style at the table on the screen porch if we weren't at Knickerbocker. Sparklers were about as exciting as at-home fireworks got in the '40s and we always had a supply ready at dusk. The neighborhood kids gathered on our large front lawn and brought their own supply of sparklers. Another popular item was "caps" which came rolled into a strip of heavy paper with miniscule amounts of gunpowder embedded sporadically. A good-sized rock was used to pound the "caps" and make a small pop.

Thanksgiving

Thanksgiving morning dawned very early for the deer hunters and for Mom, too. Dad, his brothers Frank and Will with Will's son Bob, occasionally Harold Bailey, and "the boys", would prepare for days to be ready for opening day of deer season at The Island just south of the village, or some other carefully selected nearby location. Warm camouflage clothing was readied, rifles or shot guns were cleaned and prepared, and food was readied for the hunters. Before sun-up, they were on their way to stage a full-on assault of the deer population of Schodack Island. Often, they came home empty handed, but there were many years that a deer was brought home on the roof of the car or draped over a fender of the Plymouth and then hung from the large tree just outside the back hall. Dad would arrange for the deer to be kept in cold storage until a local meat cutter was available to come to the basement and package the venison which was then distributed to all who had participated in the hunt.

A major focal point of the dining room over the years was The Deer Head. As Jack recalls, around 1953 a Crist hunting party set out during deer season to test their luck. The day was nearing its end when Bob and Jack, along with Harold and Allen Bailey, pushed a large deer to the area where Dad was waiting to meet up with them. Dad saw the deer, took aim, and had his prize—a ten-point buck. Dad had the head and neck preserved by a taxidermist and mounted on a wooden frame. The deer head hung in the dining room—at first on the backside of the bathroom wall over the buffet and later on the porch wall over a small dresser—for the remainder of the time Dad owned the house. (Although I do believe my mother would have been very happy had it hung on the outside of the porch wall!) As each grandchild came of age, say one or two years old, they would be held up beside the deer at Christmas time as they were told that Rudolph had gotten stuck! Oh no!!!! After Dad passed away, the deer head was donated—at Dad's request—to be displayed at the gate house to Schodack Island State Park where it still resides.

On Thanksgiving Day, the group would hunt until two or three p.m. and then head home to clean up in time for dinner. Sometimes the hunting party stopped at a local downtown "establishment" to warm up on the way home. This came to be known, in code language among the men, as a stop at "Mahogany Ridge."

Mom was also up very early on Thanksgiving morning to get an early start on baking the pumpkin and mincemeat pies. While the pies baked, Mom cleaned up from that effort and started making the stuffing. Day-old bread had been torn apart into a large container the previous day. Thanksgiving morning was time to add the spices, butter, water, celery, onion, and maybe an egg or two. The turkey was prepped and filled with stuffing. Neither pre-basted nor frozen birds had yet arrived on the scene, nor was aluminum foil available in the '40s. This meant that once the bird was in the oven, it required frequent basting throughout the day while Mom also busied herself with setting the table with her best Irish linen tablecloth and napkins, her Noritake "Gotham" (gold) pattern china and her prize possession: sterling flatware by Lunt in the William and Mary pattern.

Readying the turnips and cooking the giblets for a separate pot of giblet gravy were part of the routine and a special treat for Dad. Peeling a pot full of white potatoes for later mashing took time and preparing vegetables like carrots and peas was part of the effort. Almost always, there were extra mouths to feed including Aunt Ann and family, Grandma Dennin, or perhaps the girlfriend of one of the boys in later years. Bridge chairs were squeezed in at the dining room table and a card table was often set up in the living room to accommodate extra guests.

With dinner on the table, Pops carved the bird as the children were instructed not to take all the stuffing/drumsticks/corn/gravy/cranberrysauce/whatever and to leave some for the next person.

After the dinner ended and the pies were eaten, the men took to the living room to rest and visit while Mom headed back to the kitchen to wash all the dirty dishes and pots and pans. Thankfully, there were often volunteers to help with kitchen duty after Thanksgiving dinner.

Niece Corby Crist recalls: *"Thanksgiving at Grandma's: A small house, seemingly packed beyond its bounds. Adults bantering and children getting reacquainted. A Lilliputian kitchen which magically produced a mouth-watering feast. We were crammed in and knew nothing of McMansions and bonus rooms. We were together."*

Christmas

Mom would begin shopping for gifts for the children in early December. A trip to Lodge's was always in order to purchase a supply of new underwear and socks for the boys. New dungarees were always a welcome find under the tree. A special gift or two was found under the tree for each person; for Don, maybe a couple of new model airplane kits; for Dick maybe a new basketball; for me, maybe a new doll or purse.

The tree in our youngest years was always purchased by Dad. Jack remembers Dad and Uncle Frank sold Christmas trees from a lot adjacent to Grandpa Crist's apartment house on North Allen Street in Albany. The tree, when brought home, was hidden from the kids until Christmas Eve. In the earliest years, after everyone was in bed on Christmas Eve, the tree would come out of hiding and Dad would put it up in the stand. Mom would then begin decorating the tree with well-loved ornaments and silver strands of tinsel hung one by one. This process got started around ten-thirty or eleven p.m. so that it would be a glorious surprise for the children on Christmas morning. That custom changed as we all got older and started going to Midnight Mass.

Attending Midnight Mass on Christmas Eve was a strong tradition in the family. Mom and whatever children were old enough would head over to Sacred Heart around eleven-thirty p.m. The church was always packed, and people wore their finest and bore a solemn demeanor. Tall candles on the altars flickered in the night light. High Mass began with Father Gus, wearing his finest vestments, along with his acolytes, parading down the center aisle with candles and incense, and a large gold crucifix was held high. Resounding spiritual music came from Agnes Ward's organ in the loft as Father Gus proceeded to the altar. The choir sang hymns while parishioners joined in the singing. "Oh, Come All Ye Faithful" often was the opening piece, boisterous and joyful. The Mass was invariably long, and we weren't typically back home until one-thirty a.m. or later. Dad did not go to Mass with the family but always stayed up until we were home to wish us Merry Christmas.

Gifts were not individually wrapped and tagged as they are today; rather there were five stacks of gifts spread throughout the living room which were identified by Mom as to which child was the lucky recipient.

A big Christmas Day dinner—likely a turkey—that Mom somehow managed to find time to prepare, always awaited at the end of the day.

New Year's Day

New Year's Day was traditionally a day for visiting nearby family members and passing along greetings for a fine new year. I remember everyone dressing up to drive to Albany to visit Aunt Florence, Uncle Will and Aunt Amy and/or Uncle John and Aunt Kathryn in their homes. Often Uncle Frank joined the gathering. Drinks and food were offered as the family renewed their ties.

The Seasons

Ah Spring

As the long and sometimes cruel upstate New York winter began to wind down in April, people started to venture outside more often. The winter snowpack, by now dirty with rocks and soil, old and tiresome to see, often stayed on the ground until the middle of April. Eventually, spring jackets were worn in place of heavy winter coats, winter debris was cleaned up, the gardens were readied for planting, the peony bush under the spare room window began to peek through the soil, and idle Schwinn, Huffy or Roadmaster bikes with baskets and bells came off the porch and needed to be ridden. And before long, the ever-present fly swatter was put to good use.

The porches were scrubbed down from the winter's accumulation of dirt and the cots and the glider, along with the wicker chairs for the front porch, were readied for the first warm evening. Mom was in charge of the children and the inside of the house. Dad was in charge of the gardens and the lawns, the furnace and hot water heater, as well as any inside or outside maintenance, including the car. The porches were on Mom's job description.

The sweet fragrance of Mom's lilac bushes announced the arrival of spring each year. Three enormous bushes grew just to the right of the back hall at the edge of the side yard. Two displayed classic purple-colored blooms while a third bush bore double white flowers. A magnificent purple French double lilac stood in the back yard adjacent to the screen porch and demanded that you admire its blossoms and take in its heavenly fragrance. Three old and gnarled apple trees bore beautiful and fragrant spring blossoms and provided shade for the front lawn during the summer. Dad's chestnut tree at the left side of the front yard just off the front porch followed with its own glorious blossoms while Mom's crab apple tree stood to the right of the porch. A couple of generations of kids and grandkids still remember the great fun they had climbing that chestnut tree. And always, the first sighting of a red, red robin was an exciting thing to announce to the family and anyone who would listen that spring had arrived. The mulberry tree at the end of the driveway made for some great snacking in the summer. Mulberries made an awful mess, but they sure did taste great.

Soon Dad was found each evening and on the weekends in his gardens planting and tending his vegetables. Mom equally loved her front flower garden area off the lawn where she grew zinnias, sweet peas, bachelor's buttons, marigolds, snap dragons, irises, and more.

An event that was always unexpected fun occurred when a group of twenty or so young postulants on a spring outing from the nearby Sisters of the Resurrection convent on Boltwood Avenue made their way down Benedict Street. On a rare weekend afternoon, they were permitted to take a break from their religious studies and walk down our street which was parallel to theirs. The sound of their laughter acted as an alert that they were on their way past the house and were having a great time. They each wore an all-white mid-length habit with a navy or black veil reaching the midpoint of their back. Sometimes we would hear them all the way from the convent as they played softball or other outdoor games. They sounded the same as any group of happy young women having fun which, for some reason, was always a surprise.

Summertime and The Living is Easy

Castleton and its surrounding areas were marvelous places to explore and grow as the children wiled away the summer months. School was usually over by the 23d or 24th of June, following Senior Class Night on the third Thursday when academic awards and scholarships were announced, and then Prom night on Friday. Lu Bailey and I were flower girls for brother Bob's senior prom in 1949. Dressed in long yellow tulle dresses made by Mom, we preceded the prom queen down the aisle and tossed flower petals from our baskets along the way. Baccalaureate was held on Sunday night and graduation was always on Monday night—all in the school gymnasium/auditorium. The band played "Pomp and Circumstance" as the graduating seniors (somewhere between twenty-five and forty graduates depending on the year) entered the auditorium from the front sidewalk, through the double front doors of the school, marched down the center aisle, up to the stage and took their seats. Proud relatives filled the gymnasium and the balcony. Speeches were made by local officials and graduates, awards were given, the band played, and diplomas were handed out.

When the last diploma had been awarded, the excited graduates left the auditorium to the band's rendition of "Til We Meet Again." (♩ *Smile the while we bid you fond adieu . . .*). Summer had officially begun and there were more than two months of freedom and pure fun ahead. Summer camps were rare, and organized summer sporting activities even more rare. Kids were on their own to figure out how to spend each day. The expression "play date" had yet to be invented.

Bikes were the main mode of travel for the children of Castleton, and such was the world at the time that kids were free to go wherever their bikes would take them— without worry of strangers or other dangers. This was Castleton, after all, and there were no "bad" people to worry about. The innocence was a wonderful luxury for both parents and children.

We just had to be home in time for dinner when the call, ♩ "bobbyjackyDonnydickypeggyann" would go out if we weren't home on time.

Very often, on a hot summer day, those bikes took their riders to the dam. From 2 Benedict Street, it was about a ten-minute ride out Seaman Avenue to the village limit, all on level land, and then down the Brookview Road hill to the dam which sat just a few yards off the road at the bottom of the hill. The "new" dam was the only acceptable place to swim in town. The Hudson River had become badly polluted by manufacturing plants further upriver near or beyond Albany. Fishing was not advised as the catch might kill you with industrial poisons. Additionally, it was necessary to cross the railroad tracks to get to the river, and that was not an acceptable activity. And swimming pools were something that rich people in California had; certainly no one in Castleton had such a luxury.

The dam was created by the Fort Orange Paper Company to generate power for their manufacturing plant on the River Road (Rt. 9J) just outside of town. A rather large solid cement bulkhead, maybe forty feet long and about three feet thick, sat to the left of the spillway which held the water back. The Moordener Kill (translation from the Dutch: Murderer's Creek) and also known as Brookview Creek, was a gentle freshwater stream running alongside Brookview Road and fed the dam which made for awesome swimming. The water was crisp, clear, and plenty deep. The boys would swim across to the far side, clamber up the hill to the base of a tall tree, climb the tree and find the old rope to swing out over the water twenty-five or so feet below, hopefully clearing the bank on the way down. I remember once or twice seeing a boy lose his grip on the rope and fall all the way down the rock and tree encrusted hill. Oh, that had to hurt!

The telephone pole near the road had a wire that crossed over to the bank on the far side and that also presented great temptation for the boys. After climbing the pole, the boys dangled as they moved themselves along, hand over hand on the wire, to the center of the creek, and then dropped into the water below. Dangerous? Of course. But I never recall hearing of any serious injury. Another highly questionable activity was arm-wrestling on the top of the bulkhead while trying to push someone into the water. Needless to say, wrestling on top of a narrow cement bulkhead, with a drop on one side into rocky terrain thirty feet below, wasn't the smartest thing the kids ever did. But once again, to my knowledge, no one was ever badly injured.

Further down the creek, was the "old" dam also owned by the Fort Orange. This was in an isolated, hard-to-get-to location. The boys used this spot for skinny dipping while keeping a careful eye out for poison ivy. It goes without saying, we girls never knew about this secret area and wouldn't have gone there if we did know about it!

No lifeguard was ever on duty, nor were there typically any adults around to oversee the horseplay. But the kids spent countless hours there and had a great time. Eventually, hunger pangs set in and kids rode their bikes back home in the hopes that they might find something good to snack on before dinner (maybe a few Freihofer's chocolate chip cookies?).

An interesting side note is that in 1958, the year of my graduation, an act of vandalism caused the telephone wires to be broken and fall into the water below. This unfortunate event resulted in the dam being closed forever to swimmers. A very sad loss for the villagers. Today, the dam no longer exists. The Fort Orange Paper Company closed years ago, and the stream and swimming area slowly filled with silt over the years.

Sometimes in the evenings after dinner, the bikes would come out again for a trip over to Amsler's for an ice cream cone or other treat. Or maybe just to meet some friends at the school playground or tennis courts. Sitting on the porch in the still of the evening was a fine way to end the day while visiting quietly with family or friends.

With school out for the summer, the boys had lots of time to engage in active physical play—sometimes in the small living room at 2 Benedict Street. It was because of this energetic game playing that another quote from Dad became part of the family lore: "Horseplay on the front lawn!" meant, "Knock it off and quit bothering me. Go play outside."

Summertime sleepovers on the screen porch were legendary. Mom would say later in life that she never knew who to expect at the breakfast table. Lu Bailey spent many nights on our screen porch, as I spent many nights on her porch where we listened for the night sounds of the crickets singing and hoped for a gentle rain to lull us to sleep. The boys' friends, Ray Shortsleeve, Rodney Williams, Matty Bleadow, Allen Bailey, and many others often bunked overnight on the cots on the screen porch.

Pick-up baseball games out on the street, hide and seek, kick the can, red Rover come over and, of course, cowboys and Indians, filled the long summer hours. Blind man's bluff was a great game for the front porch on a rainy day. The girls especially enjoyed jumping rope as we sang the many popular rhythmic jingles of the day, including: *Sea shells, cockle shells, eevie ivy over* and *Susie and Johnny sitting in a tree. K.i.s.s.i.n.g. How many kisses did she receive? One, two . . .*

The camaraderie of the neighborhood kids was taken for granted. Judy and Geoff McDonald, their half-sister Sherry LaMarche, the Baileys, the Hardy boys (Bobby, Byron and Rodger), the Wodtkes (Gail, Wayne and Paul) and more all magically appeared, often on our front lawn, to join in the fun although we also played at their houses.

From Don: *As youngsters during and just after the war, Dick and I, along with the Cooper and Dillon kids, decided that we could build our own boats to go out on the river. I wish I had a picture of the 'scow' we built out of scrap lumber and plywood. There were half inch gaps between the boards in the hull that we 'sealed' with roofing tar! I remember 'sailing' it a number of times, and although you had to bail it out continually, and we almost got swamped once by a big ship, that little boat was a lot of fun for part of a summer. If only Mom and Dad had known!*

There was never a shortage of good ten cent comic books. *Superman, Batman and Robin, Blondie, Archie and Friends,* and, of course *Mickey Mouse and Friends with Uncle $crooge,* were all read on the screen porch on a lazy summer's afternoon. On a warm summer's Friday or Saturday evening, Pops could sometimes be persuaded to drive the family to the Auto Vision Drive-In in East Greenbush where a good western starring John Wayne might be playing on the outdoor screen while you watched the movie from the car. A speaker was attached to the side window and provided the sound and the snack bar was just a short walk away. On a rare occasion, Dad would set up the big 16 mm projector and movie screen from the Film Library on the screen porch after dark, invite us kids to bring a friend, and watch our favorite movie starring "Mugsy Long" or the many Laurel and Hardy movies.

One always needed to be on the alert for a sudden afternoon thunderstorm. The skies south of the river turned ashen, the wind picked up and you knew the rain wouldn't be far behind. Often it was possible to stand on the front porch and clearly watch the storm advance across the gentle, rolling skyline of the Catskill Mountains in the distance, over the river, and right up to the house. When this happened, there was a mad scramble to cover the cots on the porch and anything else that needed to stay dry (laundry on the line) and be ready for the storm. If it was a thunderstorm, the front porch provided a perfect viewpoint for watching the lightning in the mountains. The other thing that absolutely needed to happen was to rush upstairs and close the two front windows so the rain wouldn't pour into the bedrooms.

***

One summer memory was horrifying and involved the dreaded disease of polio, also known as infantile paralysis. Polio ranked very high among the most feared of illnesses before Dr. Jonas Salk's miraculous vaccine was introduced in 1955. The disease was a terrible scourge of young and old alike. If polio didn't kill its victim, it often caused permanent paralysis. Franklin Delano Roosevelt contracted polio in 1921 and never recovered the full use of his legs.

Dick was shockingly and suddenly struck with polio in the summer of 1950. Jack remembers being picked up by Mom from a summer job at the Montgomery Ward store in Albany. Mom was crying as she told Jack that Dick was in the hospital and had been diagnosed with polio. He remained in the hospital in Albany for several weeks before being permitted to return home. I remember hearing my mom tell others that each time she visited Dick, she feared that she would arrive to find him in an Iron Lung to help him breathe. To my knowledge, that was never necessary. Don remembers that Dick had lost much of his ability to use his legs following his return home on September 8, 1950. Mom worked endlessly with Dick, wrapping his legs in steaming hot towels and moving them back and forth, back and forth. All Mom's efforts and prayers were answered; Dick had a full and complete recovery, though it necessitated losing a year of school. He was a real fighter.

It also occurs to me to wonder just how Mom managed her daily visits with Dick in the hospital with four kids at home and just one car in the family. Extremely challenging for all concerned.

***

One of our most popular summertime family activities was the Sunday drive to Knickerbocker Lake. The lake was located off the State Road (as it was called) about twenty minutes away, out through the open country roads of Muitzeskill where the horses grazed behind wooden fencing and where without fail we would watch for the parrot who sat attached to a perch on the edge of a property along the route. The family spent countless wonderful Sunday afternoons at Knickerbocker Lake where the owners, Elsie and Walter Hacker, became family friends over the years. Sometimes, the Brauns would join the family at the lake bringing Grandma Dennin and the Braun family dogs along for the fun.

The lake front had a defined shallow area for new or non-swimmers, and a floating raft with a high platform was just a few minutes swim offshore. The raft was often packed with kids of all ages jumping into the water, pushing each other and diving from the platform where Dad taught me to dive. Row boats were available for rent, and plenty of picnic tables with fire pits dotted the shoreline which was lined with large birch trees to provide shade. Best of all, perhaps, was the canteen where the double scoop vanilla ice cream cones sold for ten cents. Dick remembered a frightening incident when, as a toddler myself, I spotted a very young child lying face up on the lake bottom at the pier and alerted the adults. I have only a vague memory of this. Though the adults were terrified, I am happy to report the baby was fine.

On picnic day, after church, Mom spent an hour or so preparing her famous and delicious homemade potato salad and placed it in the refrigerator to keep it cold. Hamburgers, hot dogs, potato chips, rolls, drinks, paper products, charcoal, towels, etc. were packed and placed in the trunk of the car. After the kids were in the car and the group was well underway, most in the family remember on more than one occasion hearing Mom scream in horror, "I forgot the potato salad!" which was safely stored in the refrigerator at home.

Another unfortunate incident involving me occurred at Knickerbocker when I was a small toddler. The charcoal fire was roaring, hamburgers and hot dogs were cooked, the meal consumed, and folks were relaxing in the shade of the birch trees and enjoying the day. While waiting that mandatory endless hour after eating before the kids were allowed go back into the water, screams were heard coming from the fire pit area. I had wandered through the coals in my bare feet. Happily, to this day I have no memory of this and there were no long-lasting results.

One summer, the family took a day trip to the old Yankee Stadium in the Bronx to see the Yankees play. I was young, five or six at most, but remember it quite well. Mel Allen was the well-known long-time announcer for the Yankees and had quite a following. Somehow, I managed to obtain Mel Allen's autograph. Quite exciting for a little girl. That was my only visit to the old Yankee Stadium which was demolished in 2010.

Sometime after the Crists left the Allendorf Hill home and the Wodtkes had moved in, Ed Wodtke built a backyard playhouse for the kids. It was wood-framed and a good size. Several times over the course of the summer months when the Bailey's lived there, Lu and I, along with some of the other neighborhood kids, likely including Gail, would put on a show with reserved front-row seating (and mandatory attendance) for Mom, Marjorie Bailey and possibly Georgia Hardy, Evelyn Wodtke or Ann La Marche who were always a very appreciative audience. We hung a sheet across the middle of the playhouse to make a private staging area for the performers and a separate area in the front for the audience. We would sing, dance and do whatever silly thing we thought would be appreciated by the "crowd." The big closing number was always "Blue Moon," sung to our heart's content with full emotion and dramatic input. (*"Blu...ue Moon, you saw me standing alone, without a dream in my heart, without a love of my own . . ."*).

***

Each summer, almost without exception, the family took a one-week vacation. Often it was scheduled for the very last week of August, which meant that the cold northern ocean or mountain lake waters had warmed to the maximum extent and sometimes one extra day could be added to the vacation for the Labor Day holiday. School always started the Tuesday after Labor Day.

Vacations over the years were always fun and always included a packed car, with either a roof carrier or a small trailer towed behind. The four boys were in the back, often with the family dog, while I sat beside my mother or on her lap in the front seat. No one had thought yet to invent seat belts. Early vacations included Indian Lake in the Adirondacks or Stockholm's Cabin on Lake Champlain in North Hero, Vermont. The men fished, and the women and kids swam, or a little of each. Other years, the family traveled to Hampton Beach in New Hampshire or Plum Island in Massachusetts. One later year we rented a beautiful new cabin called Valley Haven Lodge at the Sacandaga Reservoir in the Adirondack Mountains of upstate New York. The interior walls were knotty pine which was quite pretty. While everyone had a great time, and there was always a night out to sample the local fare, Mom was still the chief cook and bottle washer. From Hampton Beach, the family would drive north into Maine where Yoken's Seafood Restaurant and lobster awaited not far over the border. At Plum Island, fish and chips were plentiful and much enjoyed. Perhaps even more wonderful were the frappés (or as we called them back home, milk shakes) that the good people of Massachusetts had to offer.

And lastly, no summer was complete without a week or more of Mom working in a hot kitchen canning tomatoes, beans and peaches, or making homemade jellies. A precursor of today's instant pots, Mom's pressure cooker with its red zone gauge was always a scary thing for me. I don't think it ever exploded, but I do know there were a couple of close calls.

Autumn in New York

When the corn stalks finally stopped producing a daily supply of fresh ears of corn, and when they stood like mysterious withered brown sentries in the dusk of evening, a favorite activity of the neighborhood kids was playing hide and seek among the dried stalks. This was an activity that provided hours of fun in the waning days of summer.

***

Twice a year, the house was torn apart. The white curtains were removed from all seven of the living and dining room windows. The curtains were laundered, bleached, starched and placed on the wooden curtain rack—a medieval torture device, some called it. The rack was assembled on the screen porch and held only one or two full-sized curtain panels at a time. The surrounding framework contained countless small exposed tacks. The wet and starched curtain was placed on the tacks one-by-one and left to drip dry over several hours. On occasion, a spot of blood from a pricked finger appeared on the curtain and needed to be rinsed out.

At the same time, the windows were washed until they glistened, the Venetian blinds were taken down and washed in the bathtub and hung to dry on the porch clothes line (a grueling process), hardwood floors were cleaned, carpets were vacuumed, furniture was dusted, and the bathroom was scrubbed to a fare-thee-well. Everything possible was done to make the house spotless and look its best. The reason for this flourish of activity was Mom's Bridge Club ladies were about to pay a semi-annual visit.

Two card tables were placed in the living room along with eight folding chairs. Card-themed tablecloths and two blue Lenox ashtrays shaped in the form of card suits were on each table, along with the cards. Most everyone still smoked, including Mom. And most smoked

Chesterfields, because their friend, Arthur Godfrey, highly recommended them.

The ladies (regulars Mrs. Stahlbush, Mrs. Metzger, Mrs. Ryan, Viola Hacker, Eloise Hanreeder, with alternates Amelia Henck or Doris Stagg filling out the team) would arrive at seven p.m. dressed in their finest, play two rounds of bridge, gossip a bit and when the game was finished, Mom would serve tea in her collection of fluted English bone china tea cups along with a carefully prepared dessert. I loved to play waitress when I was old enough. Dad and the boys made themselves scarce for the evening. The Bridge Club dated back to the late 1930s and was active for well over thirty years with many of the original members.

The Long Cold Winter

The winters in Castleton were cold and they started early. Some years, snow arrived before Halloween and almost always by Thanksgiving. The house had been built in the late 1800s and so there were few protections against the cold other than the storm windows.

From Don: *"Before winter started, the coal man came by, and that was always interesting to me. He'd park his big truck alongside our back hall and set up a 'run' of steel troughs which would go through the cellar window and into our coal bin in the basement. Then he'd let go the 'gate', and the big chunks of coal would run into the coal bin downstairs with the most wonderful noise. What a dirty job! But Pops always knew how to make the best fire in the furnace—it would last from five a.m. until he got home in the evening."*

Wooden-framed storm windows were available for many of the windows to help keep out the cold. The two large windows in the upstairs bedrooms were a struggle to enclose. After Mom cleaned them, Dad managed to carry the heavy storm windows up the stairway with help from one of the boys, and got the job done of fixing them firmly in place before the cold weather set in. A much easier task was covering the many ground floor windows with storm windows. The dining room window that looked out up Benedict Street was never covered. The family cats knew that jumping up on that windowsill was the fastest way to gain quick year-round entrance to the house.

As mentioned earlier, there was only one source of heat for the house at 2 Benedict Street. Dad did a wonderful job of keeping the coal furnace in the basement working at peak capacity, but the further away one was from the grate, the colder the room became.

It was not at all unusual for the small windows in the upstairs bedrooms (which did not have storm windows available) to be covered with a thick coating of frost on the inside during the winter months.

On a chilly evening, one or two family members were often found sitting on a chair carefully placed over The Register. Cries of, "Mom! He's hogging the whole register!" weren't unusual.

When the first snows of the winter fell, the sleds came out. The kids would pull their sleds to the top of Benedict Street where the ride would begin, all the way down past Hammy Davis, Rodney Williams, Wodtkes, Everleths, MacDonalds, and Hardy's homes and then the ride kicked into full gear at the top of Allendorf Hill where the hill became much steeper, all the way down to Seaman Avenue with the many twists and turns the road offered— over and over again until our toes nearly froze off. Back in the house, the first and only stop, after boots, hats, gloves scarves and coats came off, was The Register and the warmth it provided. Often Mom offered a cup of steaming hot chocolate to help with the warming.

That same skating pond that caused trouble for Dad in 1937 was still in use during the years that we grew up (though it is gone now). Very often on a chilly winter evening after dinner, the kids would grab their skates, trek down the path past Bailey's and Jaros's, and across Seaman to the pond. There someone would be tending a roaring fire while we kids skated to our heart's content into the night. Such good fun.

Don remembers: *"The Hudson River. What adventures you could have there. In the winter, the Hudson would frequently completely freeze over; enough so that ice breaker ships regularly came through to clear a path through to Albany so that the navy's "liberty ships" could move war materials made in upstate New York down to New York City, and then to Europe or Asia. That frozen river was a huge lure to adventurous young boys. Bob and Jack on several occasions took Dick and I out on the ice and crossed over to the west shore. Down south of Castleton in the Catskill Mountains, men were working at several mines to get the natural cement that was abundant in the area. They would frequently use a blast of dynamite to break the cement loose. With WW II going on, it wasn't very hard for Bob and Jack to convince Dick and Don that the explosions we heard were actually the sounds of the war in Europe, and that we, in fact, were somehow crossing on the ice over to Germany! I'll guarantee that we kept a sharp look out for German soldiers while we were 'over there.' Another fortunate thing: the ice breaker never came through while we were in Germany."*

Those frigid upstate New York winter nights took a toll on cars with no garage to protect them from the biting winds. Pops, however, had the answer to preventing a dead battery in the morning. Before retiring at midnight, Dad took his "trouble" light outside and plugged it into a heavy-duty extension cord which was, in turn, attached to the ceiling light fixture in the back hall. The light was then placed under the hood of our brown 1939 Plymouth to assure the car would start the next morning. A heavy army blanket over the hood finished the job of keeping the motor oil from freezing and the car started very nicely in the morning.

Pops had spent his entire life enduring the hardships of cold upstate New York winters and understood what actions were necessary to keep the family comfortable.

Photographic History

Mary Besch Crist, Michael Robert Crist,
John, Will and Florence Crist

Michael and Mary Besch Crist with Dad on the left and Uncle John

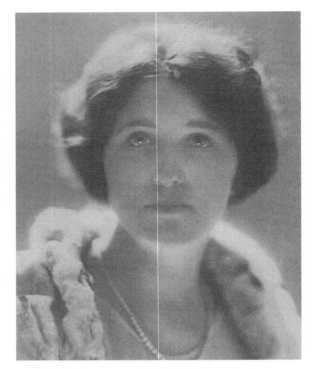

Margaret Elizabeth O'Sullivan Dennin

William and Margaret O'Sullivan Dennin

Mom and Uncle Bill Dennin

Dad (seated second on left)

Dad and Bugler

Mom and Dad on Troop B horses

Mom's wedding portrait

Bob, Jack and the Twins

Lu Bailey and me dressed for prom

The Twins at Sacred Heart

The Robert Crist Siblings

The Brauns, Mom, Grandma and Dick

Uncle Bill Dennin

Uncle John Dennin

Grandma Dennin

Grandpa Crist

At the Hofbrau Haus in Munich

John and Peg in Wiesbaden

Pops' 100th Birthday Party

Pops and Craig

Following page - Crist Family Reunion 2011

Part Three

The Rest of the Story

And so the years went by with the five Crist kids growing, getting sick, getting into trouble, attending Castleton Union School, going to Friday night Canteens at school to hang out with friends and dance (the night was officially over when they played ♫ *"Goodnight Sweetheart, w...ell it's time to go,"*) having girlfriends or boyfriends, becoming active in their classrooms or sports, graduating and thinking about what would come next. By the time I became a teenager, a local phone number to talk with my friends without a toll charge was vital to my survival, so Mom and Dad changed our Albany party line to a Castleton number (732-7894.) Area codes were not yet in use. A pink wall phone replaced the black table phone and hung beside the basement stairway where the cord thankfully still reached to the top step for privacy. Mom even went back to work for the state for a few years. She got an offer to work as a "key punch operator" (a precursor of computing). She loved the change and getting out of the house. I loved having the house to myself for a couple of hours after school and helped to get dinner started.

Each of the Crist children ultimately has been blessed with good and long lives and produced amazing children whom I am immensely proud to call my nieces and nephews. There are no words to say how proud John and I are of our own children Jennifer (and Tyler), Tim, and Megan (and Jack), and our beautiful and perfect-in-every-way grandchildren: Cosette, Marit, Sierra, Jack and Will. I will tell my brothers' and my stories here only in the briefest detail. That greater effort is left for someone of a younger generation.

First to leave the family homestead was **Bob**, who had graduated from Castleton Union School in 1949 as Student Council president. Bob took a job with Niagara Mohawk Power Corporation where he would have a forty-plus year career working his way up from beginner laborer to company executive. Bob married **Arlene Kull** in August of 1953 at Sacred Heart Church and they set up housekeeping in an apartment in nearby Sherwood Forest. Bob also served for many years with the New York State National Guard at Camp Drum, having received an Army deferment due to his work with Niagara Mohawk providing clean energy for the post-war housing boom. After living in the Castleton area for several years, his family moved to Youngstown, NY near Buffalo in 1965, and ultimately made their home in Oswego, New York with children **Bonnie, Michael, Bill** and **Lisa**. Bob and Arlene later divorced, and Arlene was killed in an automobile accident after the divorce. Bob married a second time in 1975 to a local Oswego girl, **Patricia Joyce**. Patty's son **David** also joined the family. Bob and Patty have been married over forty years as of this writing and still live in Oswego in the summer months. In the winter months they relocate to their home in North Ft. Myers, Florida.

Jack graduated from nearby St. John's High School and joined the United States Navy in 1951. In the late '50s, he married **Gaynell Bridenbeck**, a local Castleton girl. Jack and Gaynell had three children, **Corby, Mina,** and **Brian**. Son Brian was a victim of sudden infant death syndrome and died in infancy on June 24, 1962. Jack had a lengthy career with the Building Trades Union in Albany and as a member of the Operating Engineers was involved with building many of the leading construction achievements of the era: the billion-dollar Nelson Rockefeller South Mall project in downtown Albany, the Thruway Bridge just south of Castleton, and many more. Following a divorce in 1960, Jack married a second time to **Evelyn (Lynne) Sherman** in 1965 and they have two

children, **Kirsten** and **John**. They made their home in
Nassau, New York and for over forty years also owned and
upgraded "Brookside Cottage" in Bolton Landing on Lake
George. As of this writing, Jack and Lynne have been
married over fifty years and live in Rensselaer, New York
and still visit often in Bolton Landing where both Kirsten
and John have homes.

Don was next out the door when he left Castleton
after graduation in 1954 as class president to attend
college at Northrup Aeronautical Institute in Inglewood,
California. Don had earned his pilot's license at age
seventeen before earning his driver's license. While at
Northrup, Don's roommate, Ted Wagner, introduced Don
to his sister-in-law **Angela Ferrara**. Angie and Don were
married in San Diego in 1958.

They have two children, **David** and **Cathy**, and have
lived and made friends in many places in the United
States from San Diego to Plattsburgh, NY to Lancaster,
Ca, to Wichita, Kansas, to Sparta on Lake Mohawk in
New Jersey, to Phoenix, Arizona and currently in Port
Townsend in Washington State where they built a
beautiful home overlooking Puget Sound. Don worked for
Cessna and traveled widely throughout the world in his
job. Don and Angie celebrated their sixtieth anniversary
in July of 2018.

Don and Angie visited Castleton over the 1961 Labor
Day holiday in a unique style. In an article from the
September 17, 1961 issue of the Times Union—written
by none other than cousin Phil Joyce—it was noted that
Don and Angie made a 3,000-mile trip from San Diego to
Castleton in a rented single engine plane in twenty-eight
hours of flying time over five days.

Following graduation from Castleton High School in
1955, **Dick** served in the U. S. Army having received his
basic training at Ft. Dix in New Jersey. Following his
military duty, he attended the University of Kansas before
returning to Albany where he earned the first college
degree of his generation when he graduated from the

State University at Albany. After a short period of working in the building trades as a member of the Operating Engineers, Dick was sworn in as a New York State Trooper on October 6, 1965 and served for thirty-plus years. Early in his career as a Trooper, Dick met and married an Albany girl, **Janet Wasserbach**, in 1966. He served as a member of the State Police Governor's Detail under Governors Rockefeller, Wilson, Carey and Cuomo. As a capstone to his career, Dick was promoted to the Bureau of Criminal Investigations where he earned multiple commendations for his bravery and outstanding service.

In his spare time, he was an avid biker and hiker, fan of the New York Yankees, a longtime member of the Rensselaer Elks, the Melvin Roads American Legion, and parishioner at Holy Spirit Church. He enjoyed reading history and biographies, along with current events and politics, classic movies and art. He could always be counted on for a story, joke or recounting tales about his days on "The Job." Dick was also proud of winning a marksmanship contest at a gathering of retired law enforcement people in Florida. Janet and Dick were married for over fifty years and lived in East Greenbush for more than forty years. They have five children (**Richard, Craig, Gary, Heidi,** and **Ryan**). Like Bob and Patty, Dick and Janet spent their winters at their home in N. Fort Myers, Florida in recent years.

♥

When this work was underway, Dick was taken suddenly from the family he loved so much following surgery on July 22, 2017 at the age of eighty. New York State Troopers in formal dress uniform stood guard beside his coffin at the viewing at Jack Ray's Funeral Home. People wishing to pay their respects had to wait in line for up to two hours as representatives from the Troopers, the Elks, lifelong friends and family came to call. It was the largest turnout remembered by many villagers. Dick's love of his family, his humor, his great stories, his many acts of heroism while serving as a state Trooper, and love of the New York Yankees defined his life, and he will always be sorely missed by the entire family.

♥

I was the last to leave Castleton in 1964. In the footsteps of my mother, I attended Mildred Elley after graduation from the new Maple Hill High School in 1958 where I had been captain of the cheerleaders as a senior. With the exception of intramural sports, cheerleading was the only fully supported school sport available to girls at that time. Following graduation from Mildred Elley, my first job was with the Federal Bureau of Public Roads in Albany where I provided administrative support to the BPR which oversaw the building of the brand-new Eisenhower interstate highway system throughout New York State.

I continued in that job for six years while still living at home, but at twenty-three years of age, I was ready to move on and out on my own. I arranged a six-week tour of Europe in in the spring of 1964 with a friend from high school, Kathleen Meany. After a lot of thought before our departure for the tour, Kathleen and I decided to quit our jobs in Albany and stay on in Europe for the summer. I pre-ordered a new Volkswagen Beetle to be picked up at the factory in Wolfsburg, Germany upon completion of the tour. Following a fabulous tour of Europe, we took a train from Paris to Wolfsburg where I took possession of my Beetle, and we then spent the weekend in nearby Berlin. From Berlin, we headed to Wiesbaden, Germany in my new Bug and were nearly arrested by the East German Police—at the height of the Cold War—for illegally (and unknowingly) entering East Germany on our way to Wiesbaden. Oops!! In Wiesbaden we were met by Father Gilchrist, the Catholic Chaplain of the U.S. Air Force base and an old friend of Monsignor Conway who had referred us to him. Father Gilchrist guided us in promptly finding employment as civilians with the Headquarters for the United States Air Forces in Europe (USAFE). We were given housing in the brand-new Air Force-run Amelia Earhart Hotel where eight stories of efficiencies housed young women teachers, secretaries, and Red Cross aides.

It was in Wiesbaden that I met a handsome young man named John Francis McCloskey on a ski club trip to Austria. John was from Pittsburgh, Pennsylvania and worked as a civilian contractor for RCA, which in turn was a contractor to the Air Force. John was a "tech rep," or as he later described, a "spook." His job required mysterious trips to the far reaches of the northern European continent where he was not permitted or able to be in touch for weeks at a time.

Three years later, in July of 1967, John and I returned home to Castleton to be married at Sacred Heart. Following our wedding, we returned to Wiesbaden for two more years and welcomed baby **Jennifer** into the family in November of 1968. We returned permanently to the U.S. in the spring of 1969 and made our home in Greenbelt and later Lanham, Maryland where **Tim** joined the family in 1971 followed by **Megan** in 1973. John continued his employment with RCA which was under contract with NASA at the Goddard Space Flight Center in Greenbelt. In 1979, with John now working for the U.S. State Department, we moved into the home we built in Davidsonville, Maryland in the community of Harbor Hills where we still reside. In the tradition of my father watching for the red wing blackbirds' arrival in Castleton by March 6, our family now watches faithfully for the ospreys to return to the South River each year by March 17. And like the red wings, the magnificent ospreys never disappoint in marking the unofficial start of spring. We were fortunate to celebrate our fiftieth anniversary with a trip for the entire family to a dude ranch in Colorado. Memories to last many lifetimes were made by all.

**

With the children gone and Dad retired, Mom and Dad settled into their comfortable routines at 2 Benedict Street. Meals were bit more informal, and visiting children, grandchildren or friends were always welcome. There was always room for one (or two or three) more at Mom's dinner table, any day of the week. Chores and shopping were attended to, gardens were maintained, and life began to slow a bit.

Dad had retired in 1963 after a successful forty-three year career with the New York State Health Department. Mom loved spending time and having sleepovers with the local grandchildren: Bonnie, Michael, Bill and Lisa, until they moved out of the area. Corby and Mina were still nearby, while some of the younger grandchildren—Richard, Craig and Gary, Heidi and Ryan—joined the group. There were many great reunion parties over the years, filling the porches and lawns with family and neighbors—and always a keg or three of beer—at 2 Benedict. There were also wonderful parties at Jack and Lynne's home in the Nassau countryside. The large screened-in "summer house" at their home was hugely popular and well used, as were the grill and picnic tables nearby.

Mom also fulfilled a long-time desire to create a rose garden in the back yard. She spent long hours choosing her roses (Jackson & Perkins "Peace" was a favorite). She loved tending her many rose bushes and the garden became a signature landmark for Mom.

Mom and Dad also traveled to visit with out-of-town children when they could, and they took several trips driving to Florida in their retirement. On one trip south, they drove down through North Carolina and South Carolina into Daytona. They played some golf and, of course, swam. Then into Ft. Lauderdale and on to Key Largo and Key West. Heading north, they stopped in Naples for lunch and then headed to Bradenton to visit with old friends, the Corwiths, friends from the Tillicum days. My favorite part of Mom's description of their trip is this: "*The next day we went up to Tampa to see Busch Gardens. It is truly a wonderful thing to see. It costs a dollar to park, but everything else is free—including all the Budweiser you can drink!*"

Dad still enjoyed golfing and even persuaded Mom to give it a try. They golfed at nearby Cordial Greens Country Club. Mom never did get comfortable with the golf club. Once or twice during the winter, Pops' friends would take him ice fishing on Lake Champlain—a huge treat. Willie Lisosky, my good friend Tootsie's Dad, was a great fishing pal.

Dad's brother Will had purchased a new Ford Thunderbird in the early '60s and Will was happy to share the driving with Dad as Mom and Aunt Amy joined in for a day's drive to Vermont or out to the country where they toured and then stopped for a nice dinner out.

Adventures in Europe

Mom and Dad twice visited me in Europe. Their first visit was for six weeks (not counting months of persuasion on my part) and began in May of 1965. I was still single and had learned my way around the continent by then and wanted them to see some of the famous sights of Europe. I am including quotes from the travel diary that Mom kept on their first trip. My purpose in including the quotes, though lengthy, is that they give Mom a voice in her own words which is otherwise missing from this story. Moreover, her words are far more eloquent than anything I would write. Her words show her personality and excitement at traveling in Europe for the first time.

From the log I learned that Henry and Elly Maag (their long-time neighbors) drove Mom and Dad to J.F.K. in New York for their flight to Europe. They stopped for lunch at the Red Coach Inn. Mom also noted that Aunt Florence gave them two travel logs as a gift while Will and Amy gave them five dollars and the Joyce's gave a collapsible travel case. Their flight arrangements were made by me through the Davis Agency in Wiesbaden which chartered civilian flights for U.S. Forces in Europe and made a stop in Iceland en route. The round-trip fare was $199.

While in Wiesbaden, Mom and Dad stayed in my efficiency at the Amelia. I had been invited to bunk in with my good friend Ginny Kocur up on the eighth and top floor while my folks were in town. My efficiency, Room 620, consisted of a living area with two sofa beds, a coffee table and a desk and chair. There was a small cooking space with a hot plate and toaster, a small refrigerator, and a bathroom. Additionally, there was a good-sized balcony overlooking the beautiful city of Wiesbaden. For this accommodation, I paid thirteen dollars a month, including daily maid service. There was also a nice restaurant on the main level, along with other amenities such as a beauty salon, a convenience store, and more.

Our first adventure was a trip to Paris over Memorial Day of 1965 in my 1964 Bahama blue Volkswagen Beetle. From Mom: *"Off to Paris! We were amazed at how much the landscape reminded us of home. Very pretty country. We went thru Mainz, Kaiserslautern, Saarbrucken and over the border into France. You could tell right away we were in another country. The whole character of the country changed and also the houses. Very quaint little French towns. Very narrow streets with the houses built almost out to the road. Very drab and dirty—the barn and the house mostly one structure all running together. They were mostly kind of a dirty grey cement and not too well kept up. Many towns had a town square with a paved courtyard, and you could just imagine the Nazis standing people up against the walls of the houses and shooting them!"*

We drove from Wiesbaden to Verdun where we overnighted in a military BOQ (two dollars and fifty cents per night) and then into Paris the next morning. From Mom: *"Well–vous sommes arrivé. Paris is everything I ever thought it would be—just beautiful. What a thrill! We drove right down the Champs-Élyseés to the Arc de Triomphe. What a sight and what traffic—mad. But you would have thought Peg had been driving around Paris all her life. Our hotel was just off the Champs and close to the Arc. Very nice small hotel—very clean and very French. We rested a while, changed our clothes and went out for dinner. What a feeling strolling along the Champs past all the sidewalk cafes. Went to a nice restaurant. The menu was in French and the only thing that looked at all familiar was "steak tartare" so we ordered it. When it came we couldn't believe our eyes!!! A large patty of very raw ground beef with a raw egg in the center!!! We couldn't believe it! The expressions on our faces must have been something as a very nice French couple at the next table started laughing at us. She called the waiter back—gave him a big lingo in French—pointed to us and said "Steak!" He took those obnoxious hamburgers back and brought us minute steaks and French fries and a salad. Were we ever grateful to her! Dad took out a Kennedy half dollar and gave it to her. She didn't quite know what to think of it, but I said "Pour vous – souvenir." She was delighted and smiled and said, "Merci beaucoup!"*

Next morning early went to Notre Dame. Beautiful! Next a boat tour of the Seine. All the points of interest were talked about along the way. Next the Louvre. It would take a year to see everything here. We saw Venus de Milo, the Winged Victory, Mona Lisa and lots more. Dinner at the Grand Hotel. Excellent. Marvelous service. Then the Folies Bergere. What a show!!! I have never seen such costumes and scenery—also such a lack of costumes. Gorgeous! After the Folies, Peg said we should go to Pigalle for onion soup. This is really something to see. Beatniks and everything imaginable. The onion soup was marvelous— served in high bowls with French bread and cheese in it. Dad had a couple of snails some tourists from the States gave him. Home about 3:00. Had to get the concierge up to let us in!"

And lastly from Paris, "*Off to Montmartre bright and early. One has to see this to believe it! A square with unbelievably narrow streets branching off. Artists everywhere and souvenir stores and cafes—sidewalk mostly. Sacré-Cœur is beautiful—at the top of Montmartre overlooking the whole city. Well au Revoir to Paris.*"

Back in Wiesbaden, for Mom's birthday on June 2, I arranged to take them to a favorite local spot: the American Civilian Club. Tuxedoed and charming maître d' Leo greeted us as we were joined by my boss, Colonel Alvin Johanson, and his wife Elaine. We dined on chateaubriand and it was, as always at the "C" Club, a wonderful experience. We treated Mom to her first Irish coffee, which she loved. The "C" Club was situated in a large and elegantly renovated German home. The service was outstanding, and the tuxedoed waiters took excellent care of their guests. Following dinner, we moved over to a smaller room where a three-piece combo played dance music for the crowd.

I had taken two weeks of vacation and on June 5 we hit the road again in my Beetle, traveling south on the German Autobahn to our first overnight in Nuremburg. From Mom: "*We stayed at a very nice hotel—one of the American billeting facilities. I'll bet some big Nazi had slept in our bed!*" The next day we drove to Dachau "*the main and most interesting part is in the upper end (of the museum) where the gas chambers and crematoriums are just as they were— Horrifying!*" and then into Munich.

A stop at <u>the</u> Hofbrau Haus came next. "*Went to the Hofbrau Haus—what a place! Emmy's* [local Albany German restaurant] *in spades! Went to the lower level. We couldn't believe it. Real German band—the steins held one liter for a quarter. The place is 350 years old and has never been closed except once when it was bombed. Sat a table with a nice German lad from Stuttgart. I actually finished one of those steins of beer!!! After an absolute ball downstairs, we went up to the third floor to have dinner. Sat with a very nice American couple from Wisconsin. We* had wiener schnitzel—good! Regretfully left the Hofbrau Haus and Munich as we had to travel to Garmisch that night.

After arriving after 10 p.m. at the Eibsee Hotel, half-way up the Zugspitz Mountain, we awoke the next morning, looked out our window and couldn't believe it. There was the beautiful lake directly in front of the hotel— the mountains all around and the Zugspitz!!! I couldn't believe it. It was like a painting or a stage backdrop. It rises straight up for 10,000 feet. The hotel was real plush and had a good American breakfast on a dining porch overlooking the lake.

That evening we had dinner in town followed by a visit to a weinstube—just the quaintest, most delightful place with two very pretty waitresses in typical Bavarian dress. And then to a second weinstube where a zither player entertained the crowd. There was a group of young Germans in the booth across from us and they were having a ball—singing along with the zither. Pretty soon they invited us to join in hands with them and sing and sway along with them. Lots of fun.

Next came Innsbruck where Mom and Dad *"enjoyed the beautiful Austrian Alps"* en route. That night just by accident, *"We found a very nice restaurant in a building 350 years old and dined in the room where Mozart lived. It was all very thrilling."*

Heading further south we drove through the Brenner Pass into Cortina d'Ampezzo in the Italian Alps for lunch and then further south to Venice. We visited The Doges Palace and St. Mark's Cathedral at St. Mark's Square and took a lovely moonlight ride in a gondola. *"When I first saw the gondolas tied up at the wharf and rocking and pitching, I was sure I would be sick, but we were surprised at how nicely they rode in the water. Five gondolas lined up across and we just sort of drifted along the canals. There was a man with an accordion and another who sang all the Italian folk songs. He had a beautiful voice.*

Dad couldn't get used to going everywhere by

waterbus instead of by car. The Grand Canal is really beautiful. Wanted to go to the Lido but no time. Left about 3:30 for Florence—Michaelangelo's City. I'm going to see the David!"

In Florence we walked the magnificent Ponte Vecchio (old bridge) and visited *"beautiful art treasures at the Pitti Palace, the home of the Medici. The next morning after Mass at a nearby church of Santa Maria Novello, we went looking for The Academe where The David is. Had quite a time finding it, but with some help from local people finally there it was. Unspeakably beautiful—displayed in a special gallery designed for it. I just can't describe it. It must be seen."*

Eventually we arrived in Rome where we stayed in a pension on the outskirts of the city. Confident traveler though I was by then, Rome proved to be a much more challenging city to find my way around on the small, sometimes nameless, streets, than I had remembered. We had made a stop at the Roman Forum and parked. After touring, attempts to exit the area in my VW were not successful as we found ourselves back again and again in Vatican Square after a half-hour of driving. This led to a radical decision. Pops said we needed to call a cab, have him lead us to our Pension and then pay him. And that is exactly what we did. Problem solved!

Mom's descriptions of touring the sights of Rome are extensive and too long to include here. They were thrilled with the many familiar stops in the Eternal City including the Colosseum, the Roman Forum, Michelangelo's Pieta, the many Piazzas, the Trevi Fountain, Tivoli Gardens and more. What I will recount here was our visit to Saint Peter's Basilica which is also the last entry of Mom's travel log.

June 16: "We are going to see the Pope today! We left around nine and got out to St. Peter's around ten. The people were already gathering in the Square, so we got in line. People of about every nation were there and you could hear many languages spoken around us. Little girls in their First Communion dresses, priests and nuns from many different orders. Peg told us to just sort of drift in with people who had tickets, so we did just that (having been there, I knew we could get in without tickets if we played our cards right) and when they started to let people with tickets in, we just sort of sneaked in. The Papal Guards in uniform and ushers in red damask knee pants and swallowtail coats were directing people where to go. Those with different color tickets were in different sections. People were really crowding in. We stayed back a way as Peg said we would get a better view. We were right opposite the Papal Altar. When they finally let the people in without tickets, there was a mob. They were herded into a fenced in area in front of us which we called "the bull pen." I am sure they couldn't see anything except other heads around them. Finally, the trumpets sounded, and His Holiness Pope Paul VI was carried in in his chair. There was deafening applause and shouts of "Papa Paolo, Papa Paolo. Finally, he started to speak—first in Italian, then in French and finally in English. As he spoke in each language, there would be more clapping and shouting. When he came in, we dropped back still further until we finally could see him. I can't express what a thrill it was to see him. It was just a wonderful moment. After he had finished speaking, the Credo was sung and then he imparted the Papal Blessing to all present and their families and blessed all religious articles. People began to leave but Peg said we should edge forward as much as we could as they would carry him high in his chair so more could see him. We got quite close and had a wonderful close view of him as he passed by. I will always remember how he looked. He smiled and waved to everybody. An unforgettable experience. We had packed the car before we left the hotel so most regretfully, we left Rome. On to Pisa.

From Rome, we traveled back north on the narrow and twisty S-curved roads of the spectacular Italian Alps with villages far below, into Pisa where we stopped to tour and see the leaning tower. The next day we drove through the glorious Swiss Alps with an overnight or two in Geneva, and then back to Wiesbaden.

The final excursion that we three took together was to fly into the divided city of Berlin, which in 1965 was at the center of the Cold War. We landed at Templehoff Air Base which was under U.S. control. Tensions ran high in the world as East German citizens tried desperately to escape the confines of their closed and destitute city. As it turned out, my friend Ginny Kocur, who kindly put me up while Mom and Dad visited, dated the commander of Templehoff Air Force Base, Colonel Vince McGovern (whom she later married).

Vince was a charming man who had earned a spot in the *Guinness Book of Records* as the first person to fly a helicopter solo across the Atlantic. While in Berlin, Vince arranged for us to have a special private tour along the border with East Germany. We drove my VW along the border perimeter with the high barbed wire fences and where the many watch towers held East German VOPOs (guards) who trained their rifles on us as we passed by. Quite a memorable drive.

A separate trip through Checkpoint Charlie across the Iron Curtain into East Berlin added to the thrill of the visit. East Berlin in 1965 was a barren and forlorn landscape, devoid of people or traffic. We toured a bit and then headed back for the return trip through Checkpoint Charlie. The East German guards took great care before admitting us back into West Germany, thoroughly examining my little VW while we stood aside, looking under the car with large mirrors and dogs on leashes sniffing everywhere. All this with armed American GI's carefully watching the East Germans—each holding loaded rifles at the ready. Mom and Dad talked about that experience for years to come.

What none of us knew during their visit to Wiesbaden was that my brother Dick, by then a New York State trooper, had been critically injured in an automobile accident while on duty. The family back home made the agonizing decision not to inform Mom and Dad of how badly Dick was injured as they felt there was nothing they could do for him from such a distance. And they didn't want Mom and Dad's long-awaited European visit to be cut short. (And it is worth remembering that communications in 1965 were very different from the world of 2019, where free trans-Atlantic calls, texts, emails and the like are so easy to accomplish. It was extremely challenging and expensive to make a phone call from the states to Europe in those days). Thankfully, Dick made a full and complete recovery from his injuries following a lengthy hospital stay, and Mom and Dad eventually forgave those who kept the news from them.

***

Mom and Dad's second visit to Europe came in the spring of 1968 after I was married and by now expecting, though still working. They stayed with us at our apartment at Mathilden Strasse 4 in Wiesbaden. After they had settled in for a few days after their transatlantic flight, again with Icelandic Air, John and I drove with them in our new 1968 Volvo sedan to Berchtesgaden, Germany where Hitler's infamous "Eagle's Nest" lay hidden deep in the Alps and where we overnighted. From there, we traveled the next day to Vienna, Austria via Salzburg where we had a lunch stop and did a bit of touring. Upon arriving in Vienna, we found our hotel and set out to see the sights including the Schönbrunn Palace, the Spanish Riding School, the Opera House, and St. Stephens Cathedral. After sampling the local specialty, *Wienerschnitzel*, and enjoying some Viennese pastries, we were ready to hit the road back to Wiesbaden a couple of days later.

Early Saturday morning the following weekend, we headed to Ostend, Belgium, where we caught an overnight ferry to Dover in the United Kingdom. It was on this ferry ride that I felt the very first kick from baby

Jennifer. From Dover, we took a train to Victoria Station in London. We stayed several days in the Kensington area of London and saw all the mandatory sites including Buckingham Palace, Hyde Park, and The Tower of London among others.

A highlight of the stay was seeing Sammy Davis Jr. performing the lead in "Golden Boy" at the Palladium Theater in London's West End theater district. Additionally, Mom and I shopped at Harrods for my maternity wardrobe and shipped the outfits to our home in Wiesbaden. Clothing for my then-size 4 figure wasn't widely available in Germany. Also, shockingly from a 2019 perspective, it was not considered acceptable for visibly pregnant women to appear in public in Germany, and therefore, maternity clothing was at a premium in any size. It was not unusual for me to be openly stared at later in my pregnancy.

We traveled to Stratford-on-Avon where we stayed at the historic Shakespeare Hotel, built in the late 1400s. The hotel was classic with Tudor half-timbered design, and I recall that the floor of our upstairs hallway slanted at about ten degrees off level. The rate was five dollars per day. Pricey at the time. While in Stratford, we also visited the historic Anne Hathaway cottage with its breathtaking thatched roof. We also toured Warwick Castle which dates from 1068 and is furnished with original furniture and artwork, including John's favorite, court artist Hans Holbein's life-size portrait of Henry VIII.

From London, we traveled by train to Liverpool and then took the overnight ferry to Dublin, Ireland where we rented a car. Pops and John thoroughly enjoyed doing their part in keeping the stock of Guinness riding high by drinking plenty of their new product: Harp lager. After spending a couple of days in Dublin, we began our drive around the Irish Coast. Our first stop was Wexford where Waterford Crystal is manufactured. From Wexford, we headed westward toward Killarney, visiting Blarney Castle en route to kiss the Blarney stone where visitors must climb several stories on ancient steps to reach the Stone. To kiss the Stone, it is necessary to lie on your back as your head dangles upside down over the parapet as you grip vertical bars to prevent a fall. Meanwhile, attendants hold your feet to prevent a catastrophe of falling into an abyss. One who has kissed the Stone is said to be imbued with the gift of gab. Since I was expecting Jennifer at the time, I have always believed she received the gift of gab right along with me.

We stayed at a small and quaint hotel right on Lake Killarney and Pops quickly befriended Paddy, a local who took people fishing in his small boat. Paddy and Pops caught three trout. Somehow during the night, the three trout magically turned into four trout which were beautifully prepared and served to us as a surprise breakfast treat the next morning. Pops was thrilled. While in Killarney, we spent a day driving the Ring of Kerry past the soft green Irish countryside with great views of Kenmare Bay and the North Atlantic.

We continued northward to Galway where we watched thousands of salmon spawning in the Galway River and local fishermen trapping them. We later enjoyed a few of the perfectly prepared salmon that night at dinner before overnighting in Galway. The next morning we drove northward along the narrow Irish roads lined by ten-foot high peat bogs and huts with thatched roofs. We overnighted in a charming inn at Donegal. Then on to Belfast where we left our car and caught a ferry to Glasgow in Scotland. We again rented a car and drove north along the entire length of Loch Ness to Inverness. Sadly, Nessie did not put in an appearance for us though we tried hard to find her. We overnighted in Inverness and then drove south to Edinburgh at the Firth of Forth and toured the historic Edinburgh Castle which dominates the city's skyline from its position on Castle Rock. Festively-attired guards protect the bridge over the ancient moat.

After a day or two in Edinburgh, it was time to head

back home to Wiesbaden. We drove back to London where we returned our rental car and then traveled by train to Dover and ferry back to Ostend where our Volvo awaited our return. Wonderful times and wonderful memories for all, but especially for Mom and Dad who for years loved to tell the stories of their European adventures to anyone who would listen.

***

Mom and Dad made other trips to visit children in far-away places. The drive to Youngstown or Syracuse was easy and Bob and family hosted Mom and Dad for summer visits, winter fishing excursions, and several holidays. Additionally, Mom and Dad flew to Don and Angie's home in Wichita for Christmas, 1968. It was Dad's furthest trip 'west' ever. (Mom had been to San Diego, California in 1958 for Don and Angie's wedding and also was able to visit her brother Bill and family in Long Beach on that trip.) That Christmas was the famous Apollo 8 mission—the first time that man left Earth to fly around the moon. From Don, *"We all sat enthralled at the TV pictures—and listened to Frank Borman, Jim Lovell and Bill Anders read from the Book of Genesis."* Don remembers their visit as a great time for all, including the grandchildren David and Cathy.

Back in the "Real World"

When John and I returned permanently from Europe in May of 1969 with baby Jennifer, it was immediately apparent to me that Mom had lost considerable weight. She was very proud of her new size ten figure. John, Jennifer, and I moved into our apartment in Greenbelt, Maryland in July where we would live for two years.

On a visit back home I sat with Mom, Dad and baby Jennifer in the living room of 2 Benedict Street on July 21, 1969 as we watched Neil Armstrong and Buzz Aldrin's thrilling moon landing as it was described by a breathless

Walter Cronkite. We heard Armstrong utter his immortal words: *"That's one step for a man, one giant leap for mankind"* as he became the first human being to set foot on the moon.

When Mom called me in Greenbelt in August, she wanted me to know that she was "just going in for a little surgery and that I shouldn't worry." I worried. A lot. I immediately called Dr. Gebhart, the doctor we now called our own. In the context of today's HIPPA laws, it was an amazing conversation. Because he knew me, he openly shared as kindly as he knew how that Mom was facing an advanced terminal illness. It was without a doubt the worst day of my life when I realized the full enormity of what Dr. Gebhart had just told me. I fell apart—big time.

I drove to Castleton the next morning to be with the family prior to her surgery. That evening, I sat with my father and brothers at the dining room table in 2 Benedict Street and shared what Dr. Gebhart had told me. Mom had been diagnosed with advanced colo-rectal cancer. Following Mom's surgery, she began treatment for the disease with radiation. I don't think chemo was available back then as my mother never lost her hair. She courageously and **without complaint** continued with her life for two and a half years, greatly defying the odds by surviving much longer than anyone could have expected. During the course of her illness, each of her family spent as much time as possible with her. And here is the bizarre part: no one ever used the word cancer in talking with Mom during her illness. Though somewhat less so now, in the sixties, cancer was still a terrifying diagnosis and people simply didn't want to acknowledge the disease. Most with a cancer diagnosis preferred to keep the news a secret. It was just too terrible to talk about.

I moved back to 2 Benedict Street for a month or so in the summer of 1970. Jennifer (at around sixteen months old) came with me while John kept the home fires burning in Greenbelt. I did what I could to be a companion while helping to care for Mom and seeing to the household chores.

We all came together at 2 Benedict Street that Thanksgiving and I then returned to Greenbelt with John and Jennifer following the holiday. I was terribly torn between leaving Mom when she needed me or leaving John on his own at home without his family for an indefinite period.

The entire family took one last summer vacation at Lake Champlain in 1970. It was difficult knowing how much pain Mom was in, but she never complained. The trip was very bittersweet for each of us.

Mom and Dad did not have the opportunity for a lot of casual conversation during the years that we kids grew up in our small house. The need to keep the myriad operations of the household functioning along with caring for five children took much of their energy. Dad's hearing loss, combined with a lack of privacy in the home, made spontaneous and personal conversation difficult. However, during their last years together there was a visible reconnection between them. Dad realized he was going to lose the love of his life and did his best to be there for Mom in every way he knew how. In the late stages of her illness, by chance I caught a loving look that passed between them. It was a poignant moment where they silently acknowledged their love for each other and that their time together was coming to an end.

On February 6, 1971 at 5:30 in the morning in Room E604 of Albany Medical Center, Mom lost her battle with this terrible disease. She was a very youthful sixty-seven years old. To the family she left behind, it was inconceivable that she was gone. She had spent her entire life in the service of her family and loved them more than life itself. To anyone who was lucky enough to have known her, or even better, to have been one of her children, she was a saint. No one ever had a bad word to say about her. She had given her all and was gone much too soon. Her entire extended family along with family friends, friends from the village, including her bridge club ladies, filled Jack Ray's Funeral Home on Van Buren Avenue for the viewing and prayers. She wore the same pink dress that she had worn at my wedding just four short years earlier.

Mom's services the next day included a gathering for final prayers at Jack Ray's followed by a vehicle procession from the funeral home to the church she had been loyal to for over thirty-five years. A funeral Mass was followed by burial in a plot beside a lilac bush at the Sacred Heart Cemetery, where so many familiar names adorn the tombstones, including one for her grandson Brian Crist in close proximity. We all miss Mom greatly to this day, and many in the family (myself included) genuinely believe that Mom and Grandma Dennin, among others, continue to look out for and protect this family.

In yet another remarkable coincidence in our family story, Mom died on the same month and day that Dad's mother had died some forty-seven years earlier. Father and son had each lost their wife to colon cancer on February 6.

I love the description of my mother written at the time of Pops' 100th birthday by Angie, telling of their visits to Castleton from California: *I can remember seeing her coming out the front door, running down the steps, arms opened wide with the largest smile on her face to greet us!* This one sentence seems to present the essence of her personality and why she was loved by all. Thanks, Angie.

***

"Popsie," as he was known to all the grandchildren, continued to live at 2 Benedict Street after Mom was gone for the remainder of his life. Pops kept busy in his final years with hunting, ice fishing on Lake Champlain or Lake Ontario, golfing, gardening (by now a much smaller garden), watching New York Yankees baseball or Buffalo Bills or Giants football games, any golf tournament, family visits, reading his newspapers and keeping "the farm" under control.

In his later years, he could be seen raking leaves on the front lawn, his stooped body holding a cane in one hand to help keep his balance. Or even shoveling snow. Until his final days, I would call him every Sunday morning at ten a.m. By then his breakfast was over and he'd had a chance to glance at *The Times Union*. It was never smart to delay or interrupt one of Dad's meals. Family members knew well of Pops' need for routine in his life. Breakfast was always at seven a.m., lunch at noon and dinner at six. And once he started a meal, he was not happy to have it interrupted. Dad was interested in all the news about the family as well as what was going on in the world: the stock market, how his beloved Yankees were faring, watching Jack Nicklaus win another major golf tournament, and the political scene. And he still loved Olga's chili on a Saturday night.

Pops even had become a celebrity in the small city of Karatsu in Japan, where Megan lived for two years in the mid-90s and taught English to local school children. After hearing many stories from Megan about her remarkable grandfather, the school developed and awarded the annual "Popsie Prize," given to a Japanese student for outstanding achievement in learning English. In appreciation, Pops sent engraved "gold" medals to the winners each year.

We celebrated Dad's one hundredth birthday with him on March 6, 1999 with a dinner at Scarnatto's Restaurant in Castleton. He would only permit the five of us children and our spouses at this event. A bigger party for the entire family came later in the year at Knickerbocker Lake.

Large articles with many photographs appeared in Albany newspapers and he received congratulations and citations from President Bill Clinton, Governor George Pataki, and most state and local elected officials. Dad was still active, kept a very positive attitude, did not complain, and enjoyed life every day. His broken hip had left a shortened left leg (which he called his "game leg") and caused a considerable limp in his adult years. It was necessary for him to buy special shoes with a lift of several inches added in the left shoe to compensate for the shortened leg. But that did not hold him back. Even on the coldest days of the winter, Pops would put on his coat and hat to walk back and forth on the side porch to get his exercise.

Nearby grandchildren genuinely enjoyed visiting with him and talking baseball, football, or philosophy on living a smart life. There were great stories from the old days that Pops loved to tell. He was proud to say that as a child he had been a member of one of the first Boy Scout Troops in the country and remembered having met Sir Adam Baden-Powell, a Londoner who was the founder of the Boy Scouts. We don't know when this meeting took place or the circumstances surrounding it.

Dad also recalled another event from their early marriage years when he and Mom traveled to New York City. It was their first time to watch the Yankees play in their home stadium in The Bronx. The team that year included Number 3, Babe Ruth, and Number 4, Lou Gehrig, both icons in New York Yankees history and in the world of baseball.

Pops also told of having met and shaken hands with both Annie Oakley and Buffalo Bill Cody who traveled the country with their enormously popular Wild West show. Another story Pops told was of a former boss who had been a passenger on the ill-fated Titanic. Pops said that this man infamously dressed like a woman to get himself safely off the ship before it sank.

The five of us "children" visited whenever possible. Each day, Stan Hotaling, the town mail man (who had attended high school several years before Bob and Jack and was one of Pop's fishing buddies) delivered Pops' mail right into the house. 2 Benedict was at the end of Stan's route and he had time to have a mutually enjoyable visit with Pops as they enjoyed a glass of Pops' favorite beverage, Yates County port. (In the course of this writing, I had an opportunity to 'cold call' Stan with a question about my father. When I identified myself as 'Pappy Crist's daughter,' he knew immediately who I was. We had a great chat and caught up on a lot of family news, his and ours. At eighty-eight years old, Stan sounded more like he was sixty. It seems the thousands of miles he walked while delivering the mail to the residents of Castleton were very useful.)

Heidi helped to take care of Pops in the last year or two of his life while she pursued her nursing degree at the Albany Memorial School of Nursing. Helen Bridenbeck, a local woman from the village, shared the duties with Heidi and another woman who came in the morning to prepare his breakfast and do light housekeeping. One of them would come again in the evening to prepare and clean up from dinner. Pops fixed his own lunch and enjoyed the independence of living in his own home.

And in the tradition of his own father, Pops was invited to be the Grand Marshal of the annual Memorial Day Parade in Castleton in May of 1999 three months before his death. He loved riding in the open convertible with a large sign on the side of the car informing his audience of villagers that he was 100 years old. The oldest man in Castleton, he still had a sharp mind, and he looked forward to January 1, 2000 when he would become a man who had lived in three different centuries.

September 14, 1999 was a routine day for Dad. Heidi was with him in the morning to help him start his day and fix breakfast for him. Jack joined him in late morning for a visit and to have lunch together. Jack left after lunch to permit Pops to take his daily nap. It was sometime later that afternoon that he was suddenly gone—peacefully, in his own home, on his own terms, just the way he would have preferred. Though he was 100 years old, it was still a shock to all that he was gone so suddenly. He had witnessed the dawn of electricity, horseless carriages, radio and television, air travel, the space age and the digital age. Pops had stoically survived a life-threatening illness, a severe hearing loss, a broken hip, children with serious illnesses, The Great Depression, two World Wars, losing his wife and much more. In talking about the difficulties he endured, he would often say, "You take what comes your way." He would live just three and a half months short of witnessing the turn of the twenty-first century.

Like Mom's some twenty-eight years earlier, Dad's funeral was at Jack Ray's, now located on Seaman Avenue—the same home that once housed our dentist's home and office and where I played as a child. Many family members spoke lovingly of the life that Pops had lived and of his special connection to them. Dad was buried beside Mom in the Sacred Heart Cemetery.

Dad always kept small caramel candies on hand in the kitchen cabinet for when his sweet tooth spoke to him. At the funeral home, I surreptitiously snuck a few of his caramels into the casket in case Dad had a craving for sweets on his long journey ahead. Rob outlived all his siblings, their spouses, and many of his nieces and nephews.

His grandchildren remembered him as a friend, a role model, a teacher, mentor, and teller of great stories who was always interested in the lives of others. David Crist's wife Donna described him as *"the man who could inspire a thirty-year old single man (David) to travel 3,000 miles to visit him."*

***

In 2010, I, along with several members of the family, visited the Cathedral of the Immaculate Conception in Albany where we had the opportunity to talk with Father Pape, the rector of the cathedral at the time. We explained that our parents had been married in the Cathedral eighty-some years earlier in 1928 and we would love to just stand in the spot where they would have been married. Father gladly escorted us into the cathedral, past the altar rail to the left of the main altar where he unlocked the door to what was called Saint Anne's Chapel at the time and now serves as the sacristy. As we entered, a lovely fireplace stood out in the corner of the room. Father Pape said they would have stood in front of the fireplace as they took their vows all those years ago. A very moving visit indeed.

Two interesting side notes happened during our visit. The first was to learn that Bishop John Francis McCloskey, who commissioned the construction of the cathedral back in the 1840s, had studied at Mount Saint Mary's College in Maryland and graduated in 1826. 160 years later a young woman by the name of Jennifer Ann McCloskey enrolled at the same Mount Saint Mary's College. We attended her graduation from the Mount in 1993. Later in his career, after attaining the priesthood in the Diocese of New York, Father McCloskey was named the first President of Fordham University in 1841 by one of his former teachers at Mount Saint Mary's, Bishop John Hughes. Nephews Craig, Gary and Ryan would matriculate some 130 or 140 years later at Fordham. Bishop McCloskey ultimately was named the first American cardinal.

The other interesting side note from our visit to the Cathedral was, in conversation with Father Pape, I learned that he was the relative of Connie Pape, a woman I had worked with in Albany some fifty years earlier. It definitely is a small world.

The cathedral still stands on Eagle Street and continues to undergo a major renovation. Sadly, however, the church has lost many of its parishioners to the general decline in church attendance in the twenty-first century and the loss of many of the nearby homes to development.

Rob and Marge both worked very hard throughout their lifetimes, in very different ways. They also had lots of fun with family gatherings, vacations and travel. Rob was the provider while Marge was the nurturer. They traveled a long way together from those early days of playing the mandolin on the Capitol roof. There were extreme challenges, but there was always the love of family to sustain them.

Mom and Dad were not perfect, nor were their lives. But then, whose is? There were terrible illnesses over the years: tuberculosis for Dad, hepatitis A for Don and me, polio for Dick, Mom's cancer and more. There were hard times—it wasn't easy supporting five children on one income. But they endured and prevailed over devastating events. In the end, they left fifty-four direct descendants (as of this writing) behind to cherish their memory.

Closing Thoughts

In writing this story I learned a great deal about world history, Irish history, Albany history, Castleton history, and family history. The time frame of my writing coincided with the 100th anniversary of two historic events, each of which impacted our family: the end of World War I in November of 1918 and the world-wide scourge of the Spanish flu during which we lost our grandfather. And we near the 100th anniversaries of the successful conclusion of the Women's Right to Vote movement in 1920, and the beginning of Prohibition, also in 1920.

I began writing the story with some pre-conceived notions about my family's history: that we were a family of very limited means for generations; and that the women, especially my Grandmother Dennin and my mother, had toiled in excessive ways and suffered great tragedies, and that life was terribly hard.

Only some of those thoughts proved to be correct. My great-grandparents, Patrick and Bridget Dennin, who left famine and poverty behind in Ireland, successfully achieved a comfortable life in their new country. They lived in a fine three-story brick home in Albany with their large family. Great-grandfather Michael O'Sullivan owned a successful grocery business in downtown Albany in the late 1800s. Grandfather William Dennin had an influential position with the State of New York in Albany when he married my grandmother, Margaret, in 1899; and in walking the upscale street near the Capitol building where they lived, my opinion of their status changed. These were solid middle-class people and likely quite comfortable in their lifestyle.

Moreover, my grandfather, Michael Crist, was the owner of a hotel! By the time he owned it, its best days were somewhat behind it, but it was still a busy and notable place. Eventually Michael converted the hotel into a respected apartment house. Michael had also been an entrepreneur over the years, dipping his toes into various enterprises from cigar manufacture to boxing to saloon ownership and more. Again, not wealthy but definitely not poverty-stricken.

Lastly the women. One of my prime motivations in writing this story was to demonstrate to generations yet unborn just how hard it was to be a wife, mother and homemaker in the nineteenth and early twentieth centuries. I hope I have shown some of the challenges our female ancestors faced. However, I have also come to understand that while my female ancestors did work very hard and had great trials in their lives, I am aware that the current generation of young women—wives, moms, daughters—work just as hard as their ancestors but in vastly different ways.

I observe my daughters, my nieces, and so many young women who are "doing it all" (meaning having a great career or owning a business, but still making time to be an awesome wife, mother, daughter, and neighbor while raising children in the challenging digital age.)

So, yes, our ancestors faced challenges of infant deaths, very poor health care, being widowed at young ages all with little societal support. But the young women I am privileged to know today work just as hard in their own century and in their own way though their challenges are different. And my hat is off to each of them.

The Wrap Up

Our Grandparents

Grandma Dennin died on May 4, 1964 at ninety-three years of age. She lived on her own in a small apartment at 359 Hamilton Street in Albany where Mom would drop by for a visit on her weekly marketing trips. Grandma was a kind, but strong-willed woman who remained devoted to the Catholic church throughout her life. Her daily attendance at Mass and her faith had sustained her throughout her long life and helped her get through the sad and very difficult times. Her mind was still sharp at ninety-three. In her last days, from her hospital bed, she asked me to pray that her Lord would take her home. She had outlived her husband by an astonishing forty-five years. At ninety-three, her work was done. Her funeral was held, appropriately, at the Cathedral of the Immaculate Conception on Eagle Street in Albany just days before I left for Europe. **Grandpa William W. Dennin** died as a victim of the Spanish flu in 1918.

Rob's father **Michael** died of colon cancer in 1954 in Albany at age eighty-nine while still living alone at 1 North Allen Street. An interesting fact is that Bob and Arlene's first child, Bonnie Ann, was born August 9, 1954, the same day that Grandpa died. Rob's mother, **Mary Besch Crist**, had died at a much younger age, also of colon cancer, in 1924. Dad would have been about twenty-five when he lost his mother.

The Margaret Dennin Siblings

Two of three surviving children of William and Mary Curley Dennin, like their younger siblings, had shortened lives. Marion had moved to Elmhurst, Long Island and was employed by the City of New York. Sadly, there had been no contact for many years between Marion and her younger half-siblings. In a loving letter dated October 19, 1941, Marion replied to a letter from my mother saying how pleased she was *"after all these years to have found my family again."* She mentions having been in phone touch with brother Bill and visiting *"he and Ludy quite a little, and greatly looked forward to seeing both Marge and Ann in the near future."* Just weeks after she wrote this letter, while she was returning from church on Sunday, November 16, two cars collided on the street forcing one of the cars onto the sidewalk where Marion was walking. She was struck and killed. She was fifty-one years old. She did not live long enough to reconnect with Marge or Ann in person as she had so wanted to do.

As an adult, Edgar married Anna Schnapp in 1912, and the marriage produced four children, including Edgar, Jr., their second-born child born in 1918. Edgar served in the U.S. Army during World War II and later lived at 265 Broadway in Menands, New York where he worked as a pressman and raised four children with Anna. He died on April 27, 1951. Edgar Jr. lived on Kenwood Avenue in Delmar, New York where he became the treasurer of the Fire Department and had a forty-nine-year career as a pressman for the J. B. Lyon Company. Ed, Jr. died on March 8, 1998. Ed's son David is married to Marjie who kindly assisted in this part of the story. I had the great pleasure to meet both Marjie and David in the summer of 2019 while visiting Cooperstown, New York, where they now live.

Mom's sister, Ann, married Edmund J. Braun a year or two prior to Marge and Rob's marriage in 1928. Eddie was born on August 11, 1893 and was a U.S. Army veteran of the First World War. Ann and Eddie's first home was at 333 Mountain Street and they later moved to 7 Plymouth Avenue in Delmar. Their only child, Joanne C. Braun, was born on March 12, 1928. Marge and Ann were very close, and the families visited often.

Aunt Ann is remembered fondly. She was kind, funny and never, ever forgot to send a card to her niece and nephews on their birthdays. Each year to early adulthood, the card arrived on time and contained two crisp one-dollar bills. Given the times and her circumstances, this was a very generous gift and one that was always appreciated. Mom was sure to remind the children to acknowledge the card and gift with a thank you note.

(A side note is that Aunt Ann's best friend over the years on Plymouth Avenue was Marge Rutnick. Marge's children played with Joanne as youths. One of those children, Doug, as an adult became the father of Kirsten—who went on to marry a man by the name of Gillibrand. Senator Kirsten Gillibrand now represents New York State in the United States Senate and was a candidate for U.S. president in 2019.)

Uncle Eddie served for twenty-five years as an auditor with the Internal Revenue Service in Albany, following an earlier career with an Albany bank. He retired in 1963. He was a great piano player and enjoyed visiting Rob and Marge where a piano was available to him. Following Eddie's death on September 7, 1968, at age seventy-five, Ann Braun and Joanne continued to live together at 7 Plymouth Avenue until Ann's death on October 26, 1986 at age eighty-six.

Joanne led a rather troubled life following her graduation from the Catholic Vincentian High School in 1945 and one year at New Rochelle College where she scored excellent grades. She never ventured into the working world and never had her own home. She was a very bright young woman but had serious social anxiety issues. She loved to read; doted on her two British Dandie Dinmont dogs, and closely followed the New York Yankees. She maintained, with her mom, a beautiful rose garden that was the envy of her neighborhood. She also spent great amounts of time and effort investigating the truth about who killed John F. Kennedy. To my knowledge, she didn't share her findings. In 1963, Joanne won a trivia contest held by a local newspaper. The prize was a new Chevrolet Biscayne auto from which Uncle Eddie derived the benefit as neither Ann nor Joanne had a driver's license. Joanne lived to age eighty-three and passed away on January 11, 2012.

Mom's brother, **Bill**, married a California girl, Katherine Lucy "Lutie" Sever. Lutie was a childhood nickname that stayed with her throughout her life. Aunt Lutie had a sophisticated, charming personality that at the same time was down to earth. She was always upbeat with a little twinkle of the devil in her eye. Bill and Lutie lived in various places such as Manhattan; Mountain Lakes, New Jersey; Denver, Indianapolis and ultimately in Long Beach, California where their sons **Bill Jr**. and **Joe** were raised. At the start of his career, Bill Sr. traveled throughout New York State and, according to Joe, sold candy. He also sold insurance for a period. Bill ultimately found success as the vice president and general manager of a company called Pacific Nik-o-lok, originally based in Indianapolis and later in Los Angeles.

In the 1940s and '50s, it was common practice for public restroom doors to bear a lock which required a nickel coin to open. Nik-o-lok manufactured many of these locks. When Uncle Bill visited over the years, he always handed out small brown leather pouches on a chain with the name Nik-o-lok etched into the leather. Inside the pouch was a nickel to assure that you would have a coin in time of need. The children were always thrilled to receive one of the pouches.

Bill bore a resemblance to Clark Gable; a handsome dark-haired man who sported a dashing mustache. His outgoing personality, deep gravelly voice, and hearty laugh made him very popular with all the family, especially his adoring older sister, Marge. All the family loved Bill's visits and looked forward to his stories about life in far away and exotic California. Bill Dennin died suddenly of a heart attack in July of 1971 at the age of sixty-seven, just six short months after my mother's death. His son, Bill Dennin Jr. died of a heart ailment known as atrial fibrillation at age forty-seven, leaving wife Sue and four children behind. Aunt Lutie died in January of 1984.

Joe Dennin celebrated his seventy-fifth birthday in 2018 and lives at this writing with his wife of more than fifty years, Sandy, in Bethesda, Maryland. Joe was awarded a Fulbright scholarship following his graduation from Stanford Law School and studied in Finland for a year. In his lengthy career as an attorney, among many interesting appointments, Joe served as Counsel to the United States Senate Select Committee on Intelligence chaired by Idaho Senator Frank Church in 1975. The committee had oversight of the Central Intelligence Agency and the National Security Agency among other agencies including the FBI and the IRS. Joe served our country for many years in the fields of international trade and finance, as well as working in private practice throughout his career. And in his spare time, he managed to visit 193 of the 195 countries officially recognized by the United States government. He's still working on getting to Somalia and Libya.

Sandy had a lengthy and successful teaching career which began in West Manhattan. Following a move to the D.C. area, she continued teaching at the Sidwell Friends School in Washington where several children of U.S. Presidents were enrolled over the years. After a record-setting twenty-five years at Sidwell, Sandy retired in 2016. Retiring faculty were recognized by the school during an end-of-year honors ceremony for graduating seniors. Sandy needed no help in recognizing the man who sat directly in front of her and turned in his seat to shake her hand when she was acknowledged. Barack Obama was in the audience as the father of a graduating senior and was happy to offer his congratulations to Sandy. Joe and Sandy's three children are Teri (Adams) of Maplewood, New Jersey; Allison of Seattle, Washington and Jimmy and his wife Caroline of Bethesda, Maryland.

John Dennin married Elizabeth Nehill, known as Betty. John and Betty lived at 152 North Pine Avenue in 1936 and ultimately made their life near Rochester in Beechwood, New York, where John earned a reputation as a tax expert with the New York State Department of Revenue and Taxation. They had no children. When John died on May 25, 1961 at the age of fifty-nine, also of a heart attack, *Time Magazine* acknowledged his passing and noted his expertise in the tax field with the State of New York. Aunt Betty died on August 18, 1979.

The Robert Crist Siblings

The eight children born to Michael and Mary Besch Crist were:

Florence Margaret was born in 1889. She married Dr. Charles A. Perry (Uncle Doc) who was born in 1888 and died in 1944 at fifty-six. Dr. Perry served in World War I. Florence had a lengthy career with the New York State Motor Vehicle Department. She and the doctor lived at 15 Danker Avenue in Albany where Florence remained until her death on May 12, 1977 at age eighty-seven. Their marriage produced no children.

William W. was born in 1891 and married Amy Roberts from Vermont. Will served in World War I. He and Amy had one son, Roberts, and after living in East Greenbush for several years, moved to 50 Van Schoick Avenue in Albany in 1936. Will had a lengthy career with the Albany Post Office. He passed away in 1971 at the age of eighty. Their son Roberts, who was also known as Mike, served in the Army Air Force as a flight navigator in World War II and flew over forty missions in the European and Pacific theaters. He survived his plane being downed in the southwest Pacific on his twentieth mission. He lived in Westport, Connecticut for more than fifty years and died at age ninety-two in Lenox, Massachusetts on September 22, 2011.

John Cuyler was born August 23, 1893. Uncle John enlisted on August 27, 1915. He became a decorated veteran of World War I and was the recipient of two United States Army citations for "conspicuous gallantry in the Battle of the Hindenberg Line in France." One citation was dated September 29, 1918, the very day that the allies breached the infamous Hindenberg Line during a massive four-day battle. The second citation was dated the following day. This victory helped to bring the war to an end just a month later. Gary tells us that that John's heroic acts took place at the Battle of St. Quinton Canal, in Bony, France where Gary has visited and paid tribute.

Brother Jack saw to it that John's heroism was acknowledged in an *Albany Times Union* article dated November 11, 2007. John, an unarmed ambulance driver and medic belonging to the New York Army National Guard's 27th Division, 107th Infantry, *"after two days of intense fighting in the midst of the battle, advanced to a shell hole through heavy enemy mortar and machine gun fire to dress the wounds of an officer"* according to the citation. *"After dusk that day, he successfully removed the officer to shelter. The next day, Crist, who had not been armed, grabbed a pistol and joined thinning ranks of troops who managed to stop the enemy's counterattack"* his second citation notes. *"The battle at the Hindenburg Line was a bloody affair. By the time the 107th was relieved, 324 of its infantrymen were killed, 874 wounded and 22 officers either died or were wounded, according to historical and military accounts."*

After the war, John became a successful builder in Albany, with many of his homes still standing today. He and his first wife, Marion, owned a home at 5 Verplanck Street before moving to 2 Croswell Street in Albany. His marriage to Marion Frost ended when Marion died on March 15, 1940 of lung cancer at age forty-three. John later married his father's brother Bill's daughter, Kathryn Crist (a first cousin). They lived at the 2 Croswell Street home until John's death of a heart attack on January 23,

1966 at age seventy-two. There were no children from either marriage.

Frank L. was born June 9, 1896. He had a short early marriage which produced no children. Frank served as a sergeant in the Army Air Squadron during World War I. He also served in the New York State National Guard during the Second World War. He later worked for the New York State Health Department and was a member of numerous civic and veterans' associations. He was the building superintendent for his father's apartment house on North Allen Street. He later lived at 199 Hamilton Avenue and finally at 15 Danker Avenue. He died on March 26, 1987 at age ninety.

Robert Michael, my father, born in 1899.

Edna was born in 1902. Edna married **Raymond Joyce** who was born in 1897. Ray served as a sergeant with the U.S. Army in World War I and later worked for the West Albany Shops, the railroad, and the Albany Police Force where, Gary tells us, Uncle Ray helped to solve one of the great crimes of the era—the notorious kidnapping of a son of one of the rulers of the Democratic party in Albany, Ed O'Connell. John was taken from his Putnam Street home. From William Kennedy: "*Young John was held for twenty-three days in Hoboken, New Jersey while his captors sought $250,000 from the O'Connell extended family on the assumption that they were rich.*"

Kennedy was told by a reliable source that "*a high-level county official opened a county safe and offered Ed O'Connell as much money as he needed to ransom his son. Ed's reply was 'Thanks a lot, but the money is coming in so fast we don't know what to do with it'.*" Eventually the O'Connells offered $40,000 and the kidnappers took it and young Johnny was released. The bills had been marked. Eight men were soon arrested and later convicted of the crime and sentenced to long prison terms.

Ray Joyce also served as a ward leader for more than

fifty years for the Democrat party in Albany. A ward leader was in some ways a shadow government official. The leader looked out for his people. If a job was needed, one was found and offered. If a widow needed food, arrangements were made. The unspoken quid pro quo was that when it was time to vote, those on the receiving end of favors were expected to turn out and vote for the chosen candidate. Edna and Ray made their home on Second Street across from Swinborn Park in Albany and later on King Avenue. Ray died in 1981 at eighty-four years old and Edna died in 1989 at age eighty-eight. Edna and Ray were the parents of twelve children.

Raymond F. Jr. was a highly decorated U.S. Army veteran who served five years of active duty with the 83rd Division, 329th Infantry in Europe during World War II. His unit crossed the Rhine and ultimately met the Russian Army at the Elbe River, just thirty miles south of Berlin. There was much rejoicing as they all knew this meant the war would soon be over. Ray was appointed the military Governor of nine German towns and received two Silver Stars and the Bronze Star for his service to the country. Ray later served for thirteen years as Treasurer of the city of Albany and was a leader in multiple civic organizations. He taught at the Christian Brothers Academy. He and wife Joan (Simonin) had six children. Ray died in 2014.

Mary was killed in an automobile accident in 1957 and had not married.

John M. (Jackie) was a bachelor and served in the U.S. Navy during World War II and the Korean War. He died in 1985.

Edna earned the rank of Lt. Cmdr. in the United States Navy. She married Don Kelly. She died in 2004 at age seventy-seven.

Philip married Mary Tessier. He served as a medic in the Korean conflict and later became a respected journalist and editor for the *Philadelphia Inquirer*.

He died in 2016 at age eighty-seven.

Florence married Phil Ladouceur and they had seven children. Phil was a sergeant in the US Army Air Forces during World War II. Florence died on December 2, 2017 at age eighty-five.

Billy was a businessman and worked for the NY State Department of Corrections. He was active in democrat politics. He was also an Army veteran and served in Korea. He married Kathleen Hall and beautifully sang, *"I'll Take You Home Again Kathleen"* in his rich Irish tenor to his bride at their wedding reception. They had three children. He died in 2005 at age seventy-two.

Veronica was next in age and is still living at this writing. She married Ernie Kavanaugh who is deceased.

Frances worked for the Albany City government and did not marry. She died in 2009.

Bobby served in the U.S. Army National Guard, worked for the Postal Service and died in 1988. He and his wife had two daughters.

Harold was prominent in the Democrat party in the city and served as the majority leader of the Albany County Legislature. He also was the business manager for the Electricians Union. The Albany County Office Building on State Street bears his name. He married Margaret Kane and they had five children. He died in 2003 at age sixty-two.

Michaela was the youngest of the twelve children and never married. She is still living as of this writing. She worked as the Social Services special projects coordinator for Albany County and has served as the president of the Blessed Sacrament School Board.

Olive was born in 1903 and lived only two years before she died of pneumonia on January 25, 1905.

Ethel was born in 1906 and married Christopher

Harte. They lived in Nassau. They had one adopted son, Gary. Ethel died on May 4, 1989.

All the Crist siblings remained in the greater Albany area throughout their lives and stayed in contact with each other.

Acknowledgements

Thanks go to my brother, Jack, who over the years has spent uncounted hours exploring the streets and cemeteries of Albany and was able to locate the former homes of many of our grandparents, aunts, uncles, cousins, as well as many of their gravesites. His painstaking research in local libraries provided crucial historical records which add immensely to this story. These efforts, along with his unmatched personal recollections of family history, have been invaluable to me. Without Jack's collaboration, this work would not exist.

Great thanks also to nephew and genealogical researcher Gary Crist who responded to numerous pleas for help in clarifying historical data and for sharing a wealth of information he has gathered through interviews, personal travel and online research. Gary's vast knowledge of our predecessors was invaluable and his willingness to read this story with a critical eye aided immeasurably in achieving a much higher level of accuracy than I could have done on my own.

I was thrilled when nephew Craig Crist solved my biggest mystery: when did Pops have tuberculosis—before his marriage or after? Craig's ingenuity and persistence paid off with the answer. Brother Don's stories of times past were terrific, and I appreciated his thorough reading of an early draft, which produced many crucial and helpful changes. I am grateful also to brothers Bob, and Dick, as well as Cousin Joe Dennin for their recollections. Niece Heidi Crist Silvestri, who cared so lovingly for my father in his last years, also contributed to our story with visits to Albany cemeteries and researching their records, in addition to on-line research.

Niece Corby's description of Thanksgiving at Grandma's brings tears to my eyes each time I read it. Additionally, Cousin Marjie Dennin shared stories and data from her research. Each contributed their recollections, corrections and good wishes.

The cover photo of 2 Benedict was taken by Don many years ago. It is a favorite of mine and I appreciate his sharing such a perfect photo. Huge thanks to Great Niece Emily Snyder for her help with creating the book's cover and to daughters Jennifer and Megan who responded to pleas of "Help!" and were able to guide me through some of the technical aspects of writing the story. John McCloskey's knowledge of Excel was hugely helpful in compiling information in an orderly fashion as well as helping with researching Ireland in the 1800s. Thanks also to Elaine Boothby, Lynne Schwartz and Troon Harrison for their guidance and careful editing of the story and Rik Hall of Wild Seas Formatting for his patient guidance in bringing this book to completion.

Mom's Most Popular Recipes

Eggs and Noodles

Purchase a bag of the widest and flattest egg noodles you can find—often called Homestyle. Cook the amount desired per package directions. Drain.

Prepare a fry pan by heating over medium heat. (If possible, use a cast iron fry pan. Teflon-coated pans just don't give the nice crust.) Melt a couple of tablespoons of stick margarine in the pan and add the cooked noodles over low-medium heat. Immediately cover the noodles with slices of cheese. (My mother used Velveeta, but I use Swiss). Be generous. After 8 – 10 minutes, when the cheese has melted into the noodles and a light crust has formed on the bottom, place a large plate over the top holding it tightly against the skillet. Flip the whole dish onto a plate, crust side up, and slide back into the fry pan with the crusty side still up. Give it a few more minutes to continue to brown.

In the meantime, crack about two eggs per person into a bowl and scramble. Add salt and pepper as desired. When the bottom side is as brown as you like, add the eggs and stir, breaking up any large clumps. Be sure to cook until the eggs are thoroughly dry.

Serve immediately.

My mother always added a can of heated stewed tomatoes as a side dish, along with a freshly made tuna salad. And this may have been the rare exception when the "no bread at dinner" rule was broken. French bread with this meal is perfect.

Enjoy!

Potato Salad

Scrub about six to eight medium sized white or yellow potatoes. Place in an inch or two of salted water, bring to a boil, cover and lower the heat to a simmer. Cook until a fork can be inserted easily into the potato (20 – 25 minutes). Remove from the heat, drain and cool a bit.

When the potatoes have cooled to the touch, peel, and cut into bite-size cubes. Immediately, while the potatoes are still warm, add a marinade as follows: ¼ cup cider vinegar, 1/4 teaspoon of dry mustard, a teaspoon of salt and pepper as desired. Blend gently and refrigerate.

While the potatoes are chilling, prepare about a cup each of diced onions and diced celery (adjust quantities as desired). Add to the chilled potatoes and combine with your favorite mayonnaise. (Mom used Kraft Spread. My family likes Hellman's.) Chill until ready to use.

Fruit Cake

3 cups currants
    3 cups raisins
    3 cups water
    3 cups sugar
    3 tsp cinnamon
    ½ lb. butter
Boil all these together for 3 minutes. Let cool, then add:
    4 cups flour
    1 ½ tsp baking soda
    3 eggs beaten light
    10 cents worth of sugared cherries*
    10 cents worth of figs, cut fine*
    1 lb. citron, cut fine
    1 Cup nut meats
    1 wine glass of wine (I use Port or Sherry)
Note: I buy a ready-mixed fruit cake fruit mix. I get in

Kresge's

*WARNING – may be more than 10 cents today!

Grease the baking pan and line with wax paper. Bake in slow oven (275° – 300°) for 2 hours. When cold, wrap in a wine cloth and let sit for 4- 6 weeks. Mom usually made her Christmas fruitcake in mid-November. (In later years, Mom used Saranwrap as the wrap, after it was invented in 1949!)

Mom's Turkey Soup
From a 1968 letter from my Mom to me:

"As to the turkey soup, I just break up the rack, add the neck and the giblets (if you don't make giblet gravy), fill the pot with cold water, some celery tops, a carrot and an onion. Cover and simmer it most of one day. Then I put it out in the cold and let the grease rise to the top and settle. The next day, I put it back on, add any meat I may have left over (including what I pull off the neck), add salt, noodles and any gravy I may have left over. I cook this slowly until the noodles are done and that's it."

I have altered that recipe slightly over the years, i.e.: When the soup has finished cooking on the first day, I strain the broth into a clean pot. I gather all the bones, etc. in the strainer and let them cool until comfortable to handle. Then I chill the cooked broth until the grease has risen and can be removed. In the meantime, I save any meat that is nice and toss the other ingredients. Sometimes I add thin sliced carrots to the broth before serving. Enjoy!

Pops' Song

Historical Information

NAME	DENNIN FAMILY				
	DOB	DOD	AGE AT DEATH	CAUSE OF DEATH	CEMETERY
Patrick Dennin, Sr.	1790	After 1855	Unknown	Unknown	St. Agnes Cemetery, Menands, NY, Section 27, Lot 51
Timothy O'Sullivan	1808	Unknown	Unknown	Unknown	Unknown
Margaret Connors O'Sullivan	1813	Unknown	Unknown	Unknown	Unknown
Bridget Dennin	1827	1912	85	Exhaustion	St. Agnes Cemetery, Menands, NY, Section 27, Lot 51
Patrick Dennin, Jr.	1831	1881	50	Railroad occupational accident	St. Agnes Cemetery, Menands, NY, Section 27, Lot 51
Michael P. O'Sullivan	1842	1913	71	Cerebral hemmorage	St. Agnes Cemetery, Section 9, Lot 83
Elizabeth Smith O'Sullivan	1843	1919	76	Nephritis	St. Agnes Cemetery, Section 9, Lot 83
William Wilford Dennin, Sr.	1857	1918	61	Spanish flu/plague	St. Agnes Cemetery, Section 9, Lot 83
Mary Curley Dennin	1860	1893	33	Tuberculosis	St. Agnes Cemetery, Section 9, Lot 83
Mary O'Sullivan	1868	1925	57	Unknown	St. Agnes Cemetery, Section 9, Lot 83
Margaret Elizabeth O'Sullivan Dennin	1870	1964	94	Old age	St. Agnes Cemetery, Section 9, Lot 83
Frank Dolan	1872	1932	60	Unknown	St. Agnes Cemetery
Anne O'Sullivan Dolan	1875	1961	86	Unknown	St. Agnes Cemetery
Timothy O'Sullivan	1884	Unknown	Unknown	Unknown	St. Agnes Cemetery, Section 9, Lot 83
Isabella Dennin	1885	1904	19	Ulcer/appendicitis	St. Agnes Cemetery
Bessie Dennin	1888	1889	1	Unknown	St. Agnes Cemetery, Section 27, Lot 51
Edgar Dennin	1889	1951	62	Unknown	St. Agnes Cemetery, Section 43, Lot 152
John Dennin	1890	1891	1	Unknown	St. Agnes Cemetery, Section 27, Lot 51
Marion Dennin	1890	1941	51	Struck by taxi on a sidewalk	St. Agnes Cemetery
Martha Dennin	1891	1893	2	Unknown	St. Agnes Cemetery, Section 27, Lot 51
Anna Dennin Braun	1900	1986	86	Old age	Our Lady Help of Christians Cemetery, Glenmont, NY
John W. Dennin	1902	1961	59	Heart attack	St. Agnes Cemetery, Section 9, Lot 83
Margaret Elizabeth Dennin Crist	1903	1971	68	Colon cancer	Sacred Heart Cemetery, Castleton on Hudson, NY
William W. Dennin, Jr.	1904	1971	67	Heart attack	All Souls Cemetery, Long Beach, California
Eileen Dolan	1905	1971	66	Unknown	St. Agnes Cemetery
Arthur Scherrer	1906	2001	95	Natural causes	St. Agnes Cemetery
Rose Mary Dennin	1907	1921	14	Sarcoma of right femur	St. Agnes Cemetery, Section 9, Lot 83
Joseph W. Dennin	1909	1925	16	Rheumatic fever/chronic myocarditis	St. Agnes Cemetery, Section 9, Lot 83
William Dennin	1933	1980	47	Atrial Fibrillation	All Souls Cemetery, Long Beach, California
Edmund Joseph Braun	1893	1968	75	Unknown	Our Lady Help of Christians Cemetery, Glenmont, NY
Lutie Sever Dennin	1893	1984		Unknown	All Souls Cemetery, Long Beach, California

NAME	DOB	DOD	AGE AT DEATH	CAUSE OF DEATH	CEMETERY
				CRIST FAMILY	
Margaret Sheerer	1794	1873	79	Unknown	St. John's Lutheran Cemetery, Honesdale, PA Plot 77
Casper Sheerer	1795	1864	69	Unknown	St. John's Lutheran Cemetery, Honesdale, PA Plot 77
Christian Christ	1816	1893	77	Unknown	St. John's Lutheran Cemetery, Honesdale, PA Plot 77
John Besch	1820	1903	83	Unknown	Eagle Hill Cemetery, Western Ave., Albany, NY Section A, Lot 20 (Eastern side)
Margaret Sheerer	1826	1907	81	Unknown	Eagle Hill Cemetery, Western Ave., Albany, NY Section A, Lot 20 (Eastern side)
Rosa Keller	1826	1896	70	Unknown	Eagle Hill Cemetery, Western Ave., Albany, NY Section A, Lot 20 (Eastern side)
Michael Robert Crist	1865	1954	89	Colon cancer	Albany Rural Cemetery, Section 111, Lot 89
Mary Besch Crist	1865	1924	58	Colon cancer	Albany Rural Cemetery, Section 111, Lot 89
Florence Crist	1889	1977	87	Respiratory failure	Albany Rural Cemetery, Section 111, Lot 144
William W. Crist	1891	1971	80	Unknown	Memory Gardens, Colonie, NY, Section 18, Lot D, Plot 3
John C. Crist	1893	1966	72	Heart attack	Albany Rural Cemetery, Section 111, Lot 89
Frank Crist	1896	1987	90	Heart attack	Albany Rural Cemetery, Section 111, Lot 144
Robert Michael Crist	1899	1999	100	Natural causes	Sacred Heart Cemetery, Castleton on Hudson, NY
Edna Crist Joyce	1902	1989	87	Old age	St. Agnes Cemetery, Albany, NY
Olive Crist	1903	1905	2	Pneumonia	Albany Rural Cemetery, Albany, NY Section 111, Lot 89
Ethel Crist Harte	1906	1989	83	Unknown	11 Old Mill Pond Road, Nassau, NY (private property)
Richard Allan Crist	1936	2017	81	Complications from surgery	St. Agnes Cemetery, Albany, NY, Section 51, Lot 3A
Brian John Crist	1962	1962	3 Months	Sudden Infant Death Syndrome	Sacred Heart Cemetery, Castleton on Hudson, NY

11:11